Karyn Henley

Cincinnati, Ohio

Published by Standard Publishing, Cincinnati, Ohio
A division of Standex International Corporation

Credits
Cover design by Brian Fowler
Interior design by Jeff Richardson
Cover and inside illustrations by Ed Koehler
Project editors, Jim Eichenberger, Ruth Frederick, Linda Ford, Bruce Stoker

07 06 05 04 03 02 5 4 3
ISBN 0-7847-1216-6
Printed in the United States of America

Table of Contents

TABLE OF CONTENTS

INTRODUCTION

The Irish poet William Butler Yeats once said, "Education is not the filling of a pail, but the lighting of a fire." In the first temple, the tent of meeting, there was a lampstand. God's instructions were, "Tell the people of Israel to bring you pure olive oil for the lampstand, so it can be kept burning continually. . . . Aaron and his sons will keep the lamps burning in the Lord's presence day and night" (Exodus 27:20, 21, NLT). Today we are God's temple (1 Corinthians 3:16). And our passion, our living love for the Lord, keeps our lampstand burning before him. (See Revelation 2:4, 5.) Our job in the spiritual education of children is to light a fire, a living, growing love for God within them.

The Foundations curriculum can help light that fire. Each of our students is a temple of God. So the goal of the Foundations curriculum is to construct within children the essential foundations upon which they can build (and sustain) a loving, thriving relationship with the Lord. To do this, the Foundations curriculum provides a thorough, step-by-step, in-depth exploration of the following foundations.

Quarter 1: Studying the Bible, The Foundation for Knowing God
Quarter 2: Salvation, The Foundation for Living with God
Quarter 3: Prayer, The Foundation for Growing Closer to God
Quarter 4: Worship, The Foundation for Loving God

This curriculum is intended for use with students in third through fifth grades. Each quarter is independent of the others, so they can be taught in any order. In fact, each quarter can be used as a single unit to fill in a 13-week study at any time of the year and can be followed or preceded by any other curriculum of your choice.

The following arrangement is a suggestion showing how the Foundations Curriculum can be taught in one year. Studying the Bible (September–November), Salvation (December–February), Prayer (March–May), Worship (June–August).

WALK THROUGH A WEEK

SCRIPTURE AND GOAL

The session begins with a Scripture and a simple goal. You may use the Scripture as a memory verse if you wish, or you may use it to support the theme for the day, reading the Scripture when you gather for the first prayer.

INTRODUCTORY ACTIVITY

You can begin your introductory activity as soon as the first student arrives, guiding others to join you as they come into your room. This activity serves two purposes. First, it gives the students something fun to do from the first moment they arrive. Second, it starts thoughts and conversations about the theme of the session. Talking is encouraged. Questions are welcome. Get to know your students. Make it your goal to discover something interesting and special about each one. Let them know that their mission is to discover more about God and about how they can get to know him better every day, so that God becomes their constant companion, their treasured friend, their awesome king.

DISCOVERY RALLY

Gather the students together as a group in preparation for the Discovery Centers.

What's the Good Word? This is a time to read the Scripture for the day. You may also sing a few songs if you want.

Challenge. This is a time to introduce the students to the theme for the day by making challenging statements or asking challenging questions.

Prayer. Choose a student to lead a prayer of blessing for the day's activities, asking God to open your hearts and teach everyone present.

DISCOVERY CENTERS

You will need either one teacher/facilitator for each center, or clearly written instructions that tell the students what they are to do in the center.

The way your class uses Discovery Centers will depend on how much time you have and how many students there are in your class.

- If you have a few students, go together to as many centers as you can in the time you have.
- If you have more than ten students and lots of time, divide into three groups. Send one group to each center and let each group rotate to a different center as they finish the activity, so that each student gets to go to each center during Discovery Center time.

- If you have more than ten students, but little time, divide into groups of three. Number off, one to three in each group. Each student #1 goes to the first center, #2 goes to the second, #3 goes to the third. After each center has completed its activity, the original groups of three come back together again to tell each other what they learned in their centers.
- Or you may choose to let all three centers do the same activity. Choose the one or two activities that you think your students will enjoy most. Divide the students into groups for centers, and once they are there, do not rotate. Instead, let each group do the one or two activities you have chosen.

DEBRIEFING QUESTIONS

If you have time, gather together as a large group at the end of the session to ask and answer questions and discuss the theme and/or other issues on the students' minds.

Review the Scripture for the day.

PRAY

You or a student may close your class time in prayer.

SUGGESTED BIBLE STUDY HELPS

This is by no means a complete list. As you look for these, you will find others that may be just as interesting and helpful.

Bible Handbooks

What the Bible Is All About, Henrietta C. Mears (Gospel Light)
What the Bible Is All About for Young Explorers, Frances Blankenbaker (Gospel Light)
The International Children's Bible Handbook, Lawrence Richards (Word)
The Baker Bible Handbook for Kids, Marek Lugowshi and Carol J. Smith (Baker)
New Unger's Bible Handbook: Student Edition, Merrill Unger (Moody)

Bible Encyclopedias

The Children's Bible Encyclopedia: The Bible Made Simple and Fun, Mark Water (Baker Books)

Bible Dictionaries

International Children's Bible Dictionary, Lynn Waller (Word)
The Baker Bible Dictionary for Kids (Baker)

Bible Fact Books

The Awesome Book of Bible Facts, Sandy Silverthorne (Harvest House)
The Baker Book of Bible People for Kids (Baker)
The Complete Book of Bible Trivia, J. Stephen Lang (Tyndale)

For Teachers and Older Students

Willmington's Bible Handbook, Harold L. Willmington (Tyndale)
Holman Topical Concordance (Holman Bible Publishers)
Holman Bible Dictionary (Holman Bible Publishers)
Children's Ministry Resource Edition (Thomas Nelson)
Manners and Customs in the Bible, Victor H. Matthews (Hendrickson)

What Is Prayer?

Scripture

"Jesus often slipped away to other places to be alone so that he could pray." Luke 5:16, ICB

Goal

Learn that prayer is communicating with God. It is a conversation that can happen anytime, anywhere, regarding anything.

INTRODUCTION

Find a cardboard box about 3 feet high with a top opening that measures at least 1 foot square. The opening can be even larger. This box will serve as your "well." Cut off any flaps at the top. You'll also need large plastic or paper picnic cups, string, scissors, a ballpoint pen, duct or electrical tape, and one small, flat, rectangular magnet for each student (from the craft section of a large discount store or from a craft store).

The students will prepare items for use in Discovery Center #1. As students arrive, give each student a large, plastic or paper picnic cup to make buckets to lower into the well. Ask the students to carefully punch two holes or slits near the top of their cups on opposite sides, using the ballpoint pen. Then the students can tie string through the holes as shown on page 10 to allow them to lower the cups into the well. Then the students should tape a magnet to the bottom of each cup with a narrow piece of duct tape or electrical tape at each end of the magnet. If you have extra time, let the students color the sides of the box to make the well look as though it's made of stones.

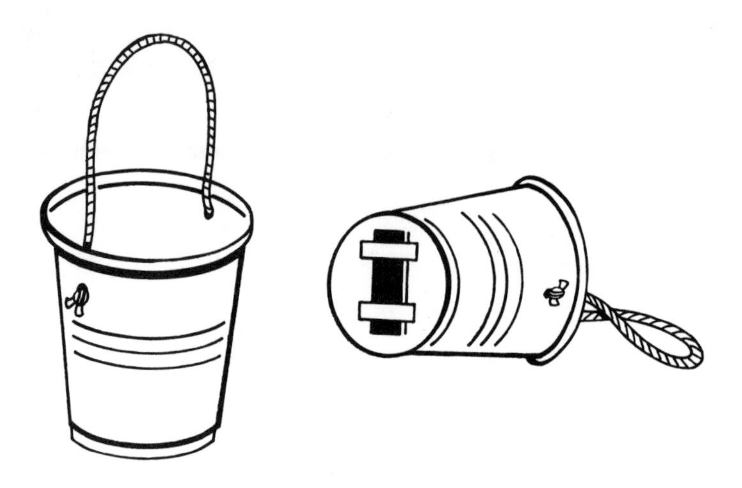

DISCOVERY RALLY

Gather students together in a large group.

WHAT'S THE GOOD WORD?

Choose a student to read the Scripture for the day.

THE CHALLENGE

Ask: **What is an experiment?** (It is trying something to see what happens.) **Have you ever heard of anyone who experimented with prayer? Long ago, in 1929, there was a missionary named Frank Laubach. He lived with his dog, Tip, close to Lake Lanao in the Philippines. He experimented with prayer.**

One thing Mr. Laubach did was to play what he called a "game with minutes." In this experiment, he tried to make a habit of having God in mind each minute he was awake. "Can I bring God back in my mind-flow every few seconds so that God shall always be in my mind . . . ? I choose to make the rest of my life an experiment in answering this question," he said.

Mr. Laubach also experimented with what he called "flash prayers." These were quick prayers that he would say as he went through his day. Once in India at a train station, he wrote, "This morning, as I came from the train and prayed for all the people on the street, I felt new energy. . . . What it does to all of them to receive that instant prayer I may never know. What is does for me is electrical. It drives out fatigue and thrills one with eager power." *(Learning the Vocabulary of*

God: A Spiritual Diary, Nashville: The Upper Room, 1956.)

Tell the students that they will learn more about prayer in their Discovery Centers today.

PRAYER

DISCOVERY CENTERS

1. THE PRAYER WELL

MATERIALS

copies of What Pray-ers Say (page 14), paper clips, buckets and well from introductory activity, paper, markers or crayons

Before the session, make copies of What Pray-ers Say. Cut apart the quotes to make separate slips. Attach a paper clip to each slip.

DO: Place the box "well" from the introductory activity at the Discovery Center location. Put all the prayer slips into the well. The students should bring the cup "buckets" they made in the introductory activity. They will take turns lowering their buckets into the well. Each student will try to pick up one prayer quote slip by positioning the cup so that the paper clip on the slip attaches to the magnet on the bottom of the cup. As the students draw out the quotes, they should read them to the group.

If you have time, the students may use colored markers or crayons to copy their quotes onto paper so they can take the quotes home.

DISCUSS: **What is prayer? People of other religions pray. What makes our prayer any different from theirs?** (First of all, prayer is like talking to a friend.) **What is the difference is between talking to the wall and talking to a friend?** (A friend listens. A friend can understand. A friend can talk back or respond. Second, prayer is speaking what's on your heart and in your mind to someone who listens, understands, and communicates back to us.) **Is there any time we *can't* pray? Is there any place we *can't* pray? Is there anything we *can't* pray about? We can pray anytime, anywhere, about anything.**

2. HOW-TO BOOKLETS

MATERIALS
white paper, crayons or markers

DO: Give each student a piece of paper. Ask the students to fold the paper in half to make a booklet. Ask the students to write "I Can Pray . . ." on the front. Then ask the students to draw and write on each page as follows:

Page 1: Draw a straight line from side to side. Draw a squiggly, wiggly line from side to side. Above the straight line write, "I can be still and pray." Above the wiggly line write, "I can move and pray."

DISCUSS: **How can you pray when you're moving? Some people pray best when they are walking or riding a bike. Some people pace the floor when they pray. What does it mean to pace the floor? Do you pray best when you are still or when you are moving?**

Page 2: Draw two eyes. Write, "I can pray with my eyes closed. I can pray with my eyes open."

How can you pray with your eyes open? Why do we usually close our eyes when we pray? Which do you think is best? Why?

Page 3: Draw around one of your hands with fingers together. Write, "I can fold my hands or I can raise my hands or I can work with my hands while I pray."

What do you do with your hands when you pray? Why would someone not fold his hands when praying? Why might someone raise his hands when praying? Also ask the students when they can or cannot pray. Ask them where they can or cannot pray. Ask them what they can or cannot pray about. **Prayer is conversation with God. It is communicating with someone who hears and answers. Why do you suppose God wants us to communicate with him?**

3. PRAYER ACROSTIC

MATERIALS
large pieces of manila paper, crayons or markers

DO: Give each student piece of paper and some crayons or colored markers. Ask the students to write the letters P, R, A, and Y in a column down the left side of their papers. Then ask each student to think of something she prays about that starts with the letter P and write it beside the P in the word PRAY. Ask the students to do the same with each letter in the word PRAY. Then they can color their pages to make posters.

DISCUSS: **What is prayer? When can we pray? What can we pray about? How can we pray? Where can we pray? Why does God want us to pray? Prayer is communicating with God. It's a conversation that can happen anytime, anywhere, about anything.**

DISCOVERERS' DEBRIEFING

If you have time to review, gather as a large group and discuss your young discoverers' findings. Ask the following questions:

- **What is the most interesting thing you discovered today?**
- **What did you learn today that you didn't know before?**
- **What is prayer?**
- **Do other religions pray? To whom do they pray?**
- **What is the difference between our prayers and the prayers of other religions?**
- **When can we pray? How can we pray? Where can we pray?**
- **What can we pray about?**

Review the Scripture for today.

Pray, thanking God for always being available to listen and to answer our prayers.

QUOTE sources for page 14

Foster—Prayer: Finding the Heart's True Home, Foster, Harper Collins
Whitman, Kenyon, MacDonald, Torrey—*Change the World School of Prayer* manual, World Literature Crusade
Juliana of Norwich, Augustine—*Prayer: Finding the Heart's True Home, by Foster,* Harper Collins
Laubach, Merton—*Streams of Living Water*, Richard J. Foster, Harper Collins
Hatchett—*Holman Bible Dictionary*, Holman Bible Publishers
MacDonald—*Change the World School of Prayer* manual, World Literature Crusade

WHAT PRAY-ERS SAY

"Real prayer comes not from gritting our teeth but from falling in love." (Richard Foster, writer and teacher)

"Prayer is doing business with God." (Virginia Whitman, author)

"Prayer means that we have come boldly into the throne room and we are standing in God's presence." (E.W. Kenyon, preacher)

"I like to think of prayer as a conversation between two friends who love and understand each other. Prayer is the key that opens the door to a whole new world." (Hope MacDonald, author)

"Prayer is the key that unlocks all the storehouses of God's . . . grace and power." (R. A. Torrey, preacher and evangelist in late 1800s and early 1900s)

"Prayer unites the soul to God." (Juliana of Norwich, lived in 1300s and spent her life praying for the world to be saved)

"Oh, this thing of keeping in constant touch with God, of making him the object of my thought and the companion of my conversations, is the most amazing thing I ever ran across." (Frank Laubach, missionary to the Phillippines, 1920s to 1940s)

"True, whole prayer is nothing but love." (Augustine, leader of the early church)

"Prayer is not so much a way to find God as a way of resting in him . . . who loves us, who is near to us." (Thomas Merton, monk who lived in early 1900s)

"Prayer makes a difference in what happens." (Randy Hatchett, university professor)

"We can read all the books that have ever been written about prayer, but until we actually choose . . . to pray, we will never learn." (Hope MacDonald)

Session 2

Great Prayers From the Bible

Scripture

"Moses and Aaron were among his [God's] priests, Samuel was among those who called on his name; they called on the Lord and he answered them." Psalm 99:6

Goal

Learn why, how, when, and where to pray by analyzing prayers of Bible-times people who communicated with God.

INTRODUCTION

Choose an area of the room where all the students can sit in one large circle. If this is not possible, divide the students into groups of eight to ten, seated in circles on the floor or at tables. As the students arrive, send them to the circle or circles to play a prayer game.

Choose one student in the group to go first. This student takes the first letter of the alphabet and uses it in the sentence: "My name is A______ and I prayed an a_________ prayer." The first blank is filled with a name beginning with the letter A, and the second blank is filled with a descriptive word (adjective) beginning with the letter A. Then the student to the first student's left says the same sentence, but this time the blanks are filled in with a name and a descriptive word that start with the letter B. The next student uses words beginning with the letter C, and so on. When they get to the letter X, they can use a word in which the second letter is X.

DISCOVERY RALLY

Gather students together in a large group.

WHAT'S THE GOOD WORD?

Choose a student to read the Scripture for today.

THE CHALLENGE

Ask: **What were some of the words used to describe prayer in our prayer game?** Using a few of those words yourself, ask students if they've ever prayed a prayer that could be described like that. **Have you ever prayed a quiet (or exciting or sleepy) prayer?** If their answer is yes, ask them what that kind of prayer is like. **Does God hear all kinds of prayers?** Tell the students that in their Discovery Centers today they will learn about different kinds of prayers and different kinds of pray-ers from Bible times.

PRAYER

DISCOVERY CENTERS

1. MURAL OF PRAY-ERS

MATERIALS
copies of Bible Pray-ers (pages 20-26), index cards, butcher paper, crayons or colored pencils, glue stick or tape

Before the session, cut out each pray-er and prayer. Tape each one to an index card to make pray-er cards.

DO: Roll out a piece of butcher paper that is about 6- to 8-feet long. Attach it to the wall at the students' eye level. Shuffle the pray-er cards facedown on a table. Let each student choose a card. Then ask each student to tape his card onto the mural. Ask the students to draw the prayer person and any other element of the description on the mural above the card using crayons or colored pencils. Remind students to leave room for the next two groups to tape their cards and draw their people.

DISCUSS: Let students take turns telling the name of the person they chose and reading the prayer that person prayed. Ask: **Why did this person pray? What kind of prayer was it?** (A prayer of gratitude, asking for help, requesting something, praying for someone else.)

2. BATTLE PRAYERS

MATERIALS
white adhesive-backed paper, half pieces of poster board, aluminum foil, tape, scissors, markers

Before the session, copy the following paraphrased battle prayers onto a chalk board, dry erase board or poster board to serve as samples for the students to copy:

"O Lord our God, deliver us from our enemy's hand, so that all kingdoms on earth may know that you alone, O Lord, are God."
King Hezekiah, 2 Kings 19:19

"O our God . . . we have no power to face this vast army that is attacking us. We do not know what to do, but our eyes are upon you."
King Jehoshaphat, 2 Chronicles 20:12

"Shall I pursue the enemy? Will I overtake them?"
David, 1 Samuel 30:8

"Do not stop crying out to the Lord our God for us, that he may rescue us from the hand of the enemy."
Israelites to Samuel, 1 Samuel 7:8

DO: Give each student a half piece of poster board. Ask each student to draw a large V shape with its point touching the center of one short side of the poster board as shown. Then the students cut this out, making a shield shape. Give the students aluminum foil and tape so they can cover their shields with silver. Then they can choose one of the battle prayers you have written. They copy their chosen battle prayer onto a sheet of white adhesive-backed paper, peel off the paper backing, and stick it onto the center of the shield.

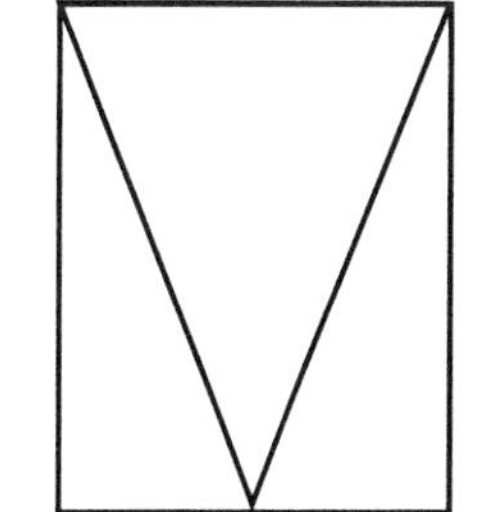

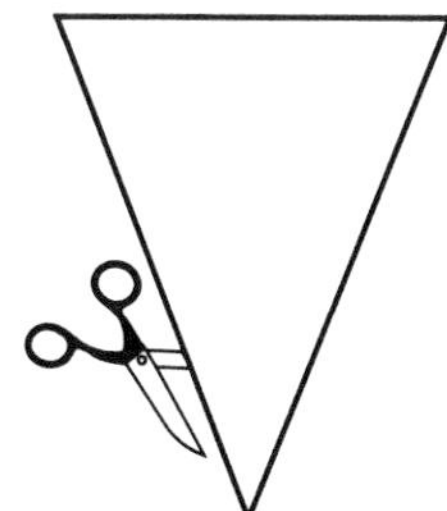

DISCUSS: As the students work, summarize what was happening at the time when each of the battle prayers was offered.

2 Kings 19:19—Hezekiah had received a letter from enemy messengers that said they would attack Jerusalem and take over the city. So Hezekiah went to the temple and spread the letter out before the Lord and prayed. That night, the angel of the Lord went through the enemy camp and killed 85,000 soldiers. So the enemy king and what was left of his army went back home. Hezekiah didn't even have to fight.

2 Chronicles 20:12—Jehoshaphat was told that a huge enemy army was headed toward him, planning to make war on God's people. All the people of Judah came together to pray. Jehoshaphat stood in front of the people and prayed. Then a prophet told Jehoshaphat to march out to face the enemy because the Lord would be with him. So Jehoshaphat set out the next morning with his army led by singers who praised the Lord. As they began to praise and sing, God came against the enemy. The enemy soldiers began to fight each other. By the time Jehoshaphat and his army got there, all the enemy soldiers had killed each other.

1 Samuel 30:8—David and his men returned home one day to find that an enemy army had raided their town and had taken away their wives and children. David prayed this prayer. God answered, "Pursue them. You will certainly overtake them and succeed in the rescue." David and his men did chase the enemy, and they rescued their wives and children.

1 Samuel 7:8—The Israelites had turned away from God, and they lost a battle with their enemy, the Philistines. Samuel told them that if they would turn back to God, God would help them fight their enemy. This verse is what they told Samuel. Samuel cried out to the Lord for the people of Israel. Meanwhile, the enemy was coming to attack. But as Samuel prayed to God, God thundered so loudly from heaven that it scared the Philistines. They panicked and ran away.

Point out that different people prayed in each situation. They prayed in different places and at different times. They did not say the same things. But God heard and answered them all.

3. WHAT'S MY NAME?

Before the session, cut out each pray-er and prayer. Tape each one to an index card to make pray-er cards.

MATERIALS
copies of Bible Pray-ers (pages 20-26), index cards, glue stick or tape

DO: Mix up the cards facedown in front of you on the table. Ask one student to draw a card but not to show it to anyone. Ask that student to read the clues about the character, but not read the name of the character. Have the other students guess who the character is. If they can't guess the person, allow them to take turns asking questions that have yes or no answers. If they can't guess the person after ten questions, tell them they are stumped, and ask the student holding the card to tell who the character is.

DISCUSS: **Why did these people pray? Where and when did they pray? How did they pray? What can we learn about praying by hearing these people's stories and their prayers?**

DISCOVERERS' DEBRIEFING

If you have time to review, gather as a large group and discuss your young discoverers' findings. Ask the following questions:

- **What is the most interesting thing you discovered today?**
- **What did you learn today that you didn't know before?**
- **What did the Bible characters pray for?**
- **What was different about each of their prayers?** (Circumstances, place they prayed.)
- **What was the same about each of their prayers?** (They asked for God's help.)
- **What can we learn from their prayers?**

Review the Scripture for today.

Pray, thanking God for hearing and answering the prayers of his people.

BIBLE PRAY-ERS

I traveled by camel caravan for a long way, looking for a girl I did not know. At last I stopped at a well and prayed, "O Lord God, give me success. When a girl comes to draw water, I'll say, 'Please give me a drink.' If she says, 'Drink. And your camels can drink too,' I'll know she's the one." Before I had even finished praying, the girl came.

Abraham's servant, Genesis 24:12-27

There was thunder and lightning, rain and hail. All the crops were beaten down by the hail. I went to see the king. "You must let God's people go," I said. "The Lord is right," said the king. "Pray to him. We've had enough hail and thunder." So I went out of the city and spread my hands out in prayer to God. Then the thunder, rain, and hail stopped.

Moses, Exodus 9:22-33 3

I was a prophet of God. I was up against 450 prophets of the false god Baal. They built an altar to Baal. I built an altar to God. All day they prayed to Baal, asking him to send fire to their altar. But nothing happened. Then I stepped forward and prayed to God, "O Lord, let these people know today that you are God. Answer me, O Lord, answer me." Then God's fire fell on his altar and burned it up.

Elijah, 1 Kings 18:19-39

I was Jewish, but I lived in Persia and was the cupbearer for the king of the Persian Empire. I had received news that the walls of the city of Jerusalem were broken down. I prayed, "O Lord, you said that if your people would obey you, you would return them to Jerusalem. Hear my prayer, and give me success today by granting me favor in the presence of the king." When I took the king's wine to him, he asked me what I wanted. I prayed and then said, "I want to go back to Jerusalem and rebuild its walls." The king allowed me to go.

Nehemiah, Nehemiah 1:1–2:6

An angel appeared to my wife and told her she would have a baby who would grow up to be a leader of God's people. I prayed, "O Lord, I beg you, let this angel come again to teach us how to raise this baby." God heard me, and the angel came again. He told us how to raise this baby.

Manoah, Samson's father, Judges 13:1-14

I was very strong, but I had been captured by the enemy. They blinded me and made me work. Then one day they brought me to a large gathering of their people, and they made fun of me. I reached out and felt the pillars that supported the building. Then I prayed, "O Lord, remember me. O God, please give me strength just one more time." Then I pushed the pillars with all my might, and the whole building fell down, killing all the enemies.

Samson, Judges 16:21-30

I had no children. I was so sad, sometimes I didn't even eat. When my husband and I went to Shiloh to worship, I went to the worship house. I prayed, "O Lord, if you will give me a son, then I will give him back to you to serve you all his life." God heard my prayer. The next year I had a son.

Hannah, 1 Samuel 1:1-20

The Israelites had turned away from God. They lost a battle with their enemy, the Philistines. I was the prophet of God who told them that if they would turn back to God, he would help them fight their enemy. They said, "Do not stop crying out to the Lord our God for us, that he may rescue us from the hand of the enemy." I did cry out to the Lord for the people of Israel. Meanwhile, the enemy marched out to attack us. But as I prayed to God, God thundered so loudly from heaven that it scared the Philistines. They panicked and ran away.

Samuel, 1 Samuel 7:3-10

I was a prophet of God. I had been leading God's people. But they wanted a king to lead them. I was not pleased. So I prayed. The Lord told me, "Listen to the people. They haven't turned away from you. They've turned away from me. Give them a king." So I did.

Samuel, 1 Samuel 8

I was a leader of some of God's people. My men and I returned home one day to find that an enemy army had raided our town and had taken away our wives and children. So I prayed, "Shall I pursue the enemy? Will I overtake them?" God answered, "Pursue them. You will certainly overtake them and succeed in the rescue." So we chased the enemy and rescued our wives and children.

David, 1 Samuel 30:3-19

I had been king of God's people for a long time. But my own son took over the throne, and I had to run for my life. Even my own counselor betrayed me and began to counsel my son. So I prayed, "O Lord, turn my counselor's advice into foolish advice." And that's just what God did.

King David, 2 Samuel 15, 17

I was the king, but I was very sick. In fact, I was about to die. I prayed, "Remember, O Lord, how I have done what is good in your eyes." Then God sent the prophet Isaiah to me with this message, "I have heard your prayer and seen your tears; I will heal you."

King Hezekiah, 2 Kings 20:1-11

I was a king of God's people. I got a letter from enemy messengers that said the enemy would attack Jerusalem and take over the city. So I went to the temple and spread the letter out before the Lord. I prayed, "O Lord our God, deliver us from our enemy's hand, so that all kingdoms on earth may know that you alone, O Lord, are God." That night, the angel of the Lord went through the enemy camp and killed 85,000 soldiers. So the enemy king and the rest of his army went back home. I didn't even have to fight.

King Hezekiah, 2 Kings 19:14-19, 35

I was king of God's people. I was told that a huge enemy army was headed toward us, planning to attack us. All the people of Judah came together to pray with me. I stood in front of the people. I prayed, "O Lord, our God, we have no power to face this vast army that is attacking us. We do not know what to do, but our eyes are upon you." Then a prophet told me to march out to face the enemy because the Lord would be with me. So I set out the next morning with my army led by singers who praised the Lord. As they began to praise and sing, God came against the enemy. The enemy soldiers began to fight each other. By the time our army got there, all the enemy soldiers had killed each other.

King Jehoshaphat, 2 Chronicles 20:2-12, 22-24

I was a prophet of God. The enemy had surrounded our city. My servant was very worried. I prayed, "O Lord, open his eyes so he may see." Then the Lord opened my servant's eyes, and he saw horses and chariots of fire filling the hills around the city. A few days later, God caused the enemy army to hear the sound of these chariots and horses. The enemy was so scared, they ran away.

Elisha, 2 Kings 6:15-17; 7:5-7

I was the most wicked king who ever ruled God's people. So God allowed me to be taken as a prisoner by the enemy. But then I realized that God was the most important. I prayed to God, and he listened to me. He allowed me to be king again.

Manasseh, 2 Chronicles 33:10-13

I was a priest and a writer. I was trying to teach God's people how to live the way God wanted them to live. But they did not obey God. So I got down on my knees and spread my hands out to the Lord. I prayed, "O my God, I am too ashamed to lift my face to you, because our sins are higher than our heads." While I was praying and crying, a large crowd of people gathered, and they began crying, too. They decided to follow God.

Ezra, Ezra 9:1–10:4

I was Jewish, but I served Darius the Mede in the kingdom of Babylon. Other men who worked for the king were jealous of me, and they planned to have me killed. They got the king to make a law that no one could pray to anyone but the king. Of course, I just went home and prayed as I always did. They trapped me. And then I was thrown into a den of lions. But God sent an angel to close the lions' mouths. After that, the king made a law that everyone had to honor God.

Daniel 6

I was a prophet who did not want to preach God's message. So I tried to run away from God. I got on a ship, thinking I would get far away. But I should have known I could not run from God. A big storm blew in, and the whole ship was in danger of sinking. At last, I told the sailors to throw me overboard. They did, and the storm stopped. But I sank into the sea. All of a sudden, I was swallowed by a huge fish. I prayed, "You brought my life up from the pit, O Lord my God. What I have promised, that I will do. You are the one who saves me." Then the fish spit me out on dry land. And I obeyed God.

Jonah, Jonah 1, 2

We were put in jail because we were teaching about Jesus. At last, we were freed. We were told that we should never again teach about Jesus. So we went back to the other believers, and we all prayed, "Lord, think about their threats and make us able to speak your word with great courage." Then the place where we were meeting shook. And we became bold!

Peter and John, Acts 4:1-31

I was hunting for Christians. I would put them in jail because they believed in Jesus. But a bright light blinded me on the road to Damascus. I went into the city, and for three days I didn't eat or drink anything. I just prayed. Then God sent a man named Ananias to me. He placed his hands on me and talked to me, and I was able to see again. Then I, too, became a believer in Jesus!

Saul/Paul, Acts 9:1-19

I was a captain in the Roman army. But I respected God. I gave to the poor, and I prayed to God. One day an angel appeared to me. The angel said, "God has heard your prayers. Send for Peter. He'll tell you what to do." So I sent some men to get Peter. He came and told me about Jesus. Then my family and I were baptized.

Cornelius, Acts 10

I was sailing in a ship, on my way to Rome, when a huge storm blew in. Our ship was tossed around on the sea for fourteen days. We knew we must be getting close to land, but it was nighttime, and we were afraid we would be dashed to pieces on the rocks. So we dropped four anchors into the water and prayed for daylight. At last, daylight came. We saw a bay and a sandy beach, so we all jumped into the sea and got to shore safely.

Paul, Acts 27:27-44

A "Handy" Way to Pray

Scripture

"Your Father knows what you need before you ask him."
Matthew 6:8

Goal

Learn a prayer pattern to use when training ourselves to pray.

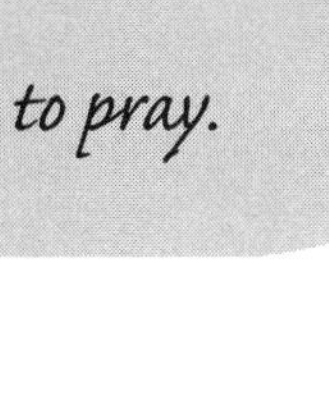

INTRODUCTION

As students arrive, give each one a copy of the Fill-in-the-Prayer handout (page 32). Ask the students to fill in the thought clouds with things they pray about. These could be things for which they're thankful, things for which they ask God's help, or names of people or countries for which they pray.

DISCOVERY RALLY

Gather students together in a large group.

WHAT'S THE GOOD WORD?

Choose a student to read the Scripture for the day.

THE CHALLENGE

Ask for volunteers to share what they drew or wrote in the thought clouds on their Fill-in-the-Prayer page from the introductory activity. Ask: **Did you have a hard time thinking of things to draw or write as prayers? Sometimes it's hard to know what we should pray about or where to start in our prayers. Even adults find it hard sometimes.** Today in the Discovery Centers, the students will find out some different ways to help them remember what to pray about.

PRAYER

DISCOVERY CENTERS

1. PRAYER BOOKLET

MATERIALS
paper, pencils with erasers, construction paper, stapler

DO: Give each student five pieces of paper, any color. Direct the students to trace around one of their hands on each page with a pencil. They may work with a partner if it's easier (one person can trace around the other person's hand). After they've traced five hands, direct the students to

- erase the little finger on one drawing
- erase the little finger and the ring finger on another page
- erase the little finger, ring finger, and middle finger on another page
- erase little finger, ring finger, middle finger, and pointer finger on another page

In place of the fingers they erased, show the students how to draw small "hills" to make knuckles, as if the fingers on the hand were folded down. Then ask students to stack the pages with the hand showing five fingers at the bottom of the stack, four fingers on top of that, three fingers on that, then the two fingers, and on top the hand with only the thumb. Staple these together at the left side to make a booklet. You can place these pages together in the center of a large piece of colored construction paper. Fold in the center, and the construction paper becomes the cover of the booklet.

Then ask the students to go through the pages and label them like this:

- thumb: Write on the hand, "People close to me." (Memory aid: the thumb is closest to you when you hold your hand up like this.)
- thumb and pointer: Draw a sad face on the fingernail area. Write on the hand, "Those in need." (Memory aid: the sad face.)
- thumb, pointer, "tall man": Write on the hand, "People in charge of me." (Memory aid: the tallest finger represents the person in authority.)
- thumb, pointer, "tall man," and ring finger (finger #4): Write on the hand, "Foreign countries." (Memory aid: 4 and **for**eign.)
- thumb, pointer, "tall man," ring finger, and small finger: Write on the hand, "Me." (Memory aid: "I am small.")

DISCUSS: As the students work, ask them questions about who these people might be. **Who are some of the people close to you? Why should you pray for these people? Who are people in need?** (The sick, the poor, the unsaved, people with problems.) **Who are the people in charge of you? Why should we pray for them? What are some foreign countries that you can pray for? Who are some missionaries you can pray for? What can you pray for about yourself?**

2. FIND-THE-COUNTRY PRAYERS

MATERIALS

cans or boxes of food, health care items, packaged paper goods, dish washing liquid or laundry detergent (but nothing chemically dangerous like drain cleaner), world map or globe

DO: Set the cans and boxes in one location in the room. Tell the students that when you say "Go," they should tiptoe to that location and choose one can or box. Tell them they must bring it back to the group. Then tell the students to examine the item and determine the location where that particular item was made. If you have a map or globe, ask the students to find that location on the globe. Then pray for that nation, state, or city.

DISCUSS: Challenge the students to pray for the countries that they see listed on products, in the news, or in books at school every day. Ask: **What are some things we can say in prayer for a nation or a people group?**

3. A CUP HAND

MATERIALS
large, disposable foam cups, pens, scissors, red string or yarn cut into 5-inch lengths

DO: Give each student a cup. Ask each student to lay her cup on its side with the opening facing her. Then ask each student to lay one hand on the cup, fingers together as if in prayer and pointing toward the bottom of the cup and the wrist at the open edge of the cup. Students should trace around their hands onto the cup. Then, beginning at the tips of the fingers (the bottom of the cup), have them cut into the cup and cut out the hand shape, but do *not* cut through the rim around the opening of the cup. The hand shape stays attached to the rim. Ask students to cut away the rest of the cup. Then have each student cut straight lines along the left and right sides of the ring finger. Give each student a piece of red string or yarn. The students slip the red string or yarn down the slits on each side of the ring finger and tie it into a bow around the base of the ring finger. Ask each student to write on the border of the cup: "Remember to pray."

DISCUSS: **Why should we pray if God already knows what we need before we ask?** Ask those who have been to Discovery Center #1 to tell you how the five fingers help them know how to pray. **Is it easy to remember to pray? If so, why? If not, why? What are some things that can help us remember to pray?**

DISCOVERERS' DEBRIEFING

If you have time to review, gather as a large group and discuss your young discoverers' findings. Ask the following questions:

- **What is the most interesting thing you discovered today?**
- **What did you learn today that you didn't know before?**
- **What is the prayer pattern that we learned by using our fingers?**
- **If God knows what we need before we ask, why do we need to pray?**

Review the Scripture for today.

Pray using the hand pattern to pray in general for God's blessings on people close to us, people in need, people in charge of us, foreign nations and missionaries, and us.

FILL IN THE PRAYER

This is you. Draw your hair.
Then fill in the thought clouds with words or drawings
that tell some things you pray about.

A Time to Pray

Scripture

"Train yourself to be godly. For physical training is of some value, but godliness has value for all things."
1 Timothy 4:7, 8

Goal

Learn another prayer pattern that can be an option to train ourselves to pray.

INTRODUCTION

As students arrive, give them a copy of the Message in a Clock handout (page 37). Ask the students to follow the directions to discover the Scripture verse for today.

Discovery Rally

DISCOVERY RALLY

Gather the students together in a large group.

WHAT'S THE GOOD WORD?

Choose a student to read the Scripture for the day.

THE CHALLENGE

Ask: **What is physical training? What does godliness mean? What might training in godliness mean? Why would training in godliness have more value than physical training?** Tell the students that we have been training ourselves to pray. Review the prayer pattern that they learned with their fingers last week. Then tell the students that we can train ourselves to pray in other ways. Today they will learn another prayer pattern.

PRAYER

Discovery Centers

DISCOVERY CENTERS

1. PRAYER CLOCK

MATERIALS
copies of the Prayer Clock handout (page 38), crayons or markers

DISCUSS: **How many minutes is a clock divided into? How many minutes come between each numeral on the clock?** Give each student a copy of the Prayer Clock handout. **Notice that this clock is divided into twelve 5-minute sections. That makes an hour.** Ask the students if they know anyone who has prayed for an hour or more. If they do, ask them to tell about this person and why and how he could pray that long. Then tell the students you'll show them how to pray for an hour (or if that's too overwhelming, use this same method to show them how to pray for 12 minutes).

DO: Ask the students to fill in the 5-minute sections of the prayer clock going clockwise with the following words:

1. Praise
2. Psalm
3. Thanks
4. Confession
5. People
6. School and studies

7. My other needs
8. My country and its leaders
9. Other countries and missionaries
10. Songs
11. Listening
12. Praise

After the students have written these into the sections, they may color the sections different colors.

DISCUSS: **In order to pray for an hour, you pray for each one of these things for 5 minutes. Even if you spend one minute doing each of these, you've prayed for 12 minutes!** As the students work, briefly discuss each of these categories. **How can praise be a part of prayer? How can a psalm help you focus on God? How can it be part of your prayer? What kinds of things are you thankful for? What if you can't think of something to confess? Can you ask God to remind you if there's a sin you need to confess? Why is confessing an important part of prayer? Who are the people you can pray about? Why should you pray about school and studies? Why is it important to pray for our leaders and our country? How can songs be part of prayer? Why should we listen for awhile when we pray?**

2. CLOCK TOWERS

MATERIALS
several empty boxes, packaging tape, paper plate, crayons or markers, colored adhesive-backed paper

DO: Let each group stack and tape together some boxes in any way they want in order to make their towers. Ask the students to draw a clock face on the highest box. (They can trace around a paper plate to make a circular clock.) Then ask them to color the clock tower with crayons or markers. Give the students sheets of colored adhesive-backed paper and let them stick squares and rectangles of colored paper on the boxes.

DISCUSS: As the students work, ask them what time of day they prefer to pray. **Is there any time when God is not listening? He never hangs out a sign that says, "Gone to Lunch" or "Closed." He's open 24 hours a day. Has anyone ever prayed in the middle of the night?** If they have, ask them to tell about it. **Tell about other unusual times you have prayed.** If you have prayed at an unusual time, tell the students about it. Tell them about your usual prayer time and why you have chosen to pray at that time.

3. PRAYER SEASONS

MATERIALS
copies of the Windows handout (page 39), crayons or markers

DO: Give each student a copy of the Windows page. Ask them to draw the view of a different season in each window: spring, summer, autumn, winter.

DISCUSS: **What might it mean to pray continually? Is that really possible? If so, how? If not, why not?** Ask the students to describe the differences between the seasons. Tell students our lives change, too. **Some people say that there are different "seasons" of life. Prayers change as our lives change. For example, how might your prayers now be different than when you learn how to drive? What might your prayers be like if you play sports on a losing team? What might your prayers be like if you play sports on a winning team? What might your prayers be like if you move to a different city? A married person is in a different "season" of life. An old person is in a different "season" of life. As you grow and change, the circumstances of your life will change, and your prayers will change. But God never changes. He listens and answers in every season. We call that being faithful. God is faithful.**

DISCOVERERS' DEBRIEFING

If you have time to review, gather as a large group and discuss your young discoverers' findings. Ask the following questions:

- **What is the most interesting thing you discovered today?**
- **What did you learn today that you didn't know before?**
- **What is the prayer pattern we learned with our hands last week?**
- **What is another prayer pattern we learned today?**
- **Why is prayer a way we can train ourselves to be godly?**
- **Why can we say that we have "seasons" in our lives?**
- **When can we pray?**
- **When does God listen?**

Review the Scripture for today.

Pray, thanking God for letting us come to him in prayer at any time. Thank him for being faithful.

MESSAGE IN A CLOCK

Fill in the blanks by writing the word at the hour that the blank matches.

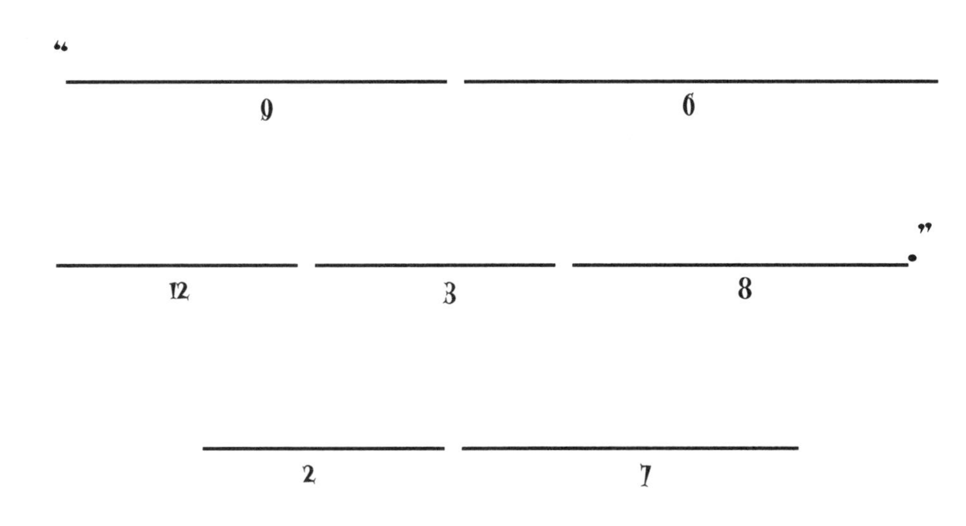

PRAYER CLOCK

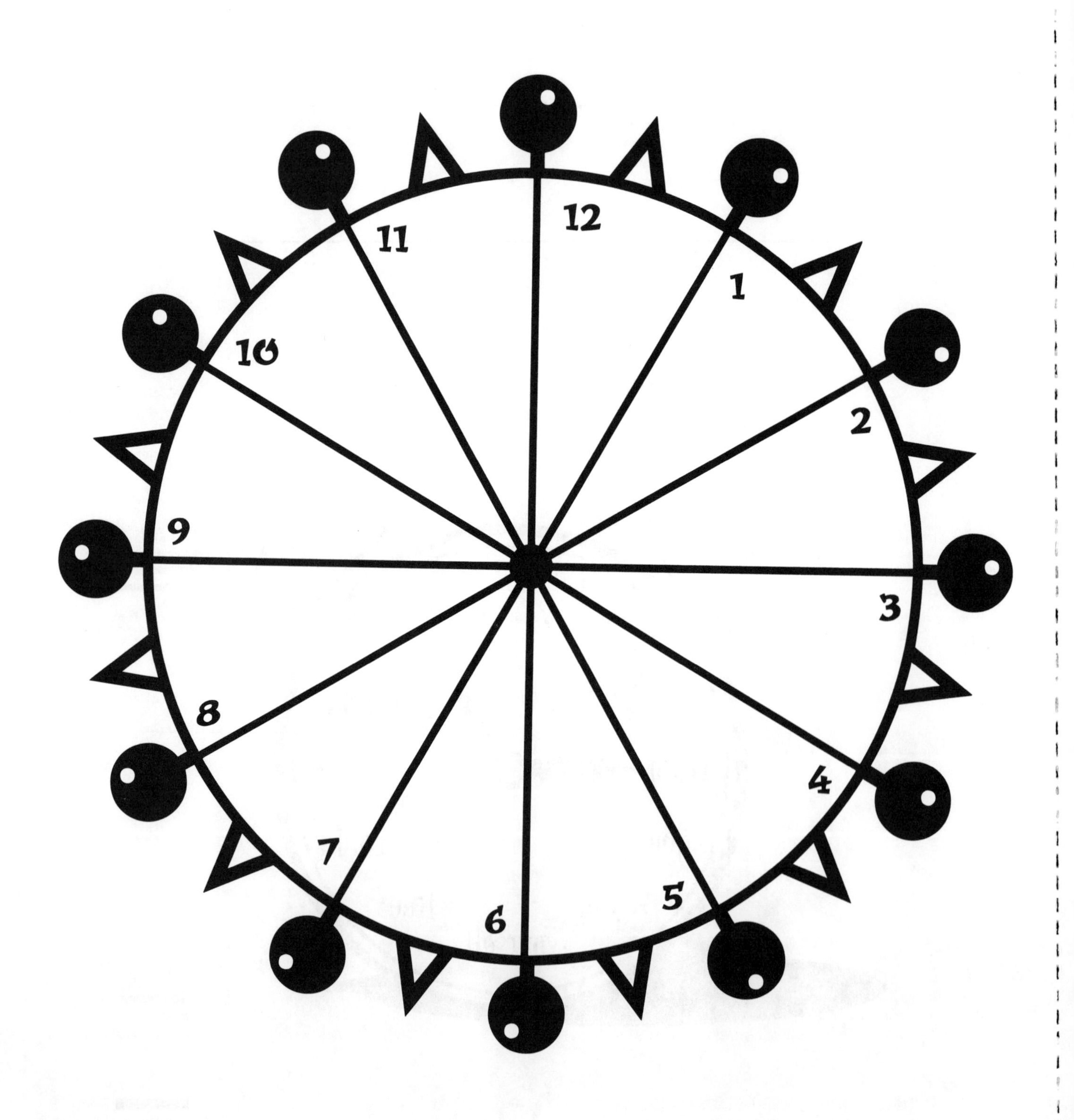

WINDOWS

"Pray continually."
1 Thessalonians 5:17

The Lord's Prayer

Scripture

"Don't worry about anything; instead, pray about everything. Tell God what you need, and thank him for all he has done."
Philippians 4:6, NLT

Goal

Learn how Jesus taught his disciples to pray.

INTRODUCTION

As the students arrive, give each a copy of the Daily Bread Bingo handout (page 45). Tell them to find classmates who fit the descriptions in the boxes. When they find one, that person must sign his name in the appropriate blank. Each classmate may sign only one blank on each sheet. Ask the students to try to fill in all the blanks in a row or column or diagonally.

DISCOVERY RALLY

Gather students together in a large group.

WHAT'S THE GOOD WORD?

Choose a student to read the Scripture for today.

THE CHALLENGE

Ask the students who completed a row, column, or diagonal to raise their hands. If you have time, ask some of them to read the names and descriptions in the completed row, column, or diagonal. Ask the students to look at the Daily Bread Bingo handout again. Ask: **How many boxes contain the name of a food that is all or partly bread? How many of you like bread? Most people like bread in some form. Ever since Old Testament times, grains and breads have been a major part of people's diets. Jesus prayed, "Give us this day our daily bread."** Tell the students that they will learn more about this prayer of Jesus in their Discovery Centers today.

PRAYER

DISCOVERY CENTERS

1. LINKING HANDS

MATERIALS
plain paper, pencils, scissors

DO: Give each student two pieces of paper. Help the students fold each piece of paper into thirds. Then ask students to unfold the papers and tape them end to end, with short ends together, making one long piece of paper. Then show the students how to use the original fold marks as guidelines, and have them fold the entire length of paper into six sections using a fan or accordion fold as shown on page 42. Next, ask the students to place their hands, with fingers together as if in prayer, on the top section of paper. The right side of the hand or finger must touch the right side of the paper, and the left side of the hand must touch the left side of the paper. Have them trace around their hands. Direct them to cut out the hand shapes through all layers of the folded paper, making sure they do not cut the area where the hands or fingers touch the edge of the paper. When they have cut out the rest of the hand, ask them to unfold the figure to show linking hands. (If this is your third group, ask them to tape the pictures they drew in Discovery Center #2 either to the palm or to the wrist of each hand. These pictures go in the order listed in Discovery Center #2.)

DISCUSS: **Each of these hands represents a part of the prayer that Jesus prayed.** Ask students to take turns reading aloud the different verses of Matthew 6:9-13. **What kinds of things did Jesus cover in this short prayer? Now, Jesus didn't always pray short prayers. For example, Luke 6:12 tells us that Jesus "spent the night praying to God."**

The students should take their paper linking hands with them to the next Discovery Center.

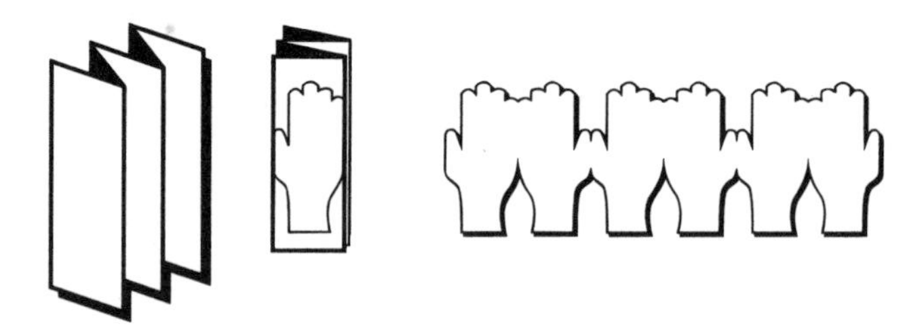

2. PAPER HAND SYMBOLS

MATERIALS
3-by-5-inch index cards (for the first group of students), paper hands from Discovery Center #1, crayons, markers

DO: Ask the students to draw objects that symbolize the sections of the Lord's Prayer on the paper hands they bring from Discovery Center #1. (Your first group will need to draw these on 3-by-5-inch index cards.)

- On the first hand, write the word *Father* and draw a star.
- On the second hand, write the word *kingdom* and draw a crown.
- On the third hand, write the word *food* and draw a piece of bread.
- On the fourth hand, write the word *forgive* and draw a cross.
- On the fifth hand, write the word *evil* and draw a frowning face.
- On the sixth hand, write the word *glory* and draw a bright light.

DISCUSS: Guide the students to say the Lord's Prayer phrase by phrase after you, looking at the symbols on each hand as they say the words of the prayer.

Star: Our Father in heaven, may your name be honored.

Crown: May your Kingdom come soon. May your will be done here on earth, just as it is in heaven.
Bread: Give us our food for today
Cross: and forgive us our sins just as we have forgiven those who have sinned against us.
Frowning face: And don't let us yield to temptation, but deliver us from the evil one.
Bright light: For yours is the kingdom and the power and the glory forever. Amen. (Matthew 6:9-13, NLT)

If you have time, ask: **How do each of the lines in the Lord's Prayer apply to us today? The book of Luke contains this prayer. It tells us that Jesus had been out praying. One of Jesus' disciples came to him and asked him to teach them how to pray. So he said this prayer to show them how to pray.** Ask the students why Jesus' disciples would ask him to teach them to pray.

3. PEANUT BUTTER HAND PRINT

MATERIALS
large flour tortillas, paper plates, peanut butter, paper towels or pre-moistened wipes

DO: Ask the students to wash their hands. Then give each student a tortilla and a paper plate. Spread a layer of peanut butter over the bottom of another paper plate. Ask the students to place their tortillas on their plates. Then ask each student to press one hand (with fingers together as if in prayer) onto the peanut butter and then onto the tortilla. Have paper towels or pre-moistened wipes ready so the students can clean their hands. After everyone has made hand prints, allow students to roll up the tortillas and eat them.

DISCUSS: **What do you think Jesus meant when he prayed, "Give us this day our daily bread?"** Ask students to name other kinds of bread (pitas, cornbread, pizza crust, pancakes.) **Why do you think Jesus would suggest that his followers pray for God to give them food? Do we need to pray this same thing today? How do we usually pray concerning food?** Ask the students if they can remember the rest of the Lord's Prayer. If not, have them say it after you. If they can remember it, ask individual students to say the Lord's Prayer.

DISCOVERERS' DEBRIEFING

If you have time to review, gather as a large group and discuss your young discoverers' findings. Ask the following questions:

- **What is the most interesting thing you discovered today?**
- **What did you learn today that you didn't know before?**
- **What did Jesus tell his disciples to pray about?**
- **Why do you think Jesus' disciples asked him to teach them to pray?**
- **If someone asked you to teach them how to pray, what would you say?**

Review the Scripture for today.

Pray the Lord's Prayer together.

DAILY BREAD BINGO

Likes coffee	Hates spinach	Likes squash	Likes broccoli
Likes cake better than cookies	Likes potato chips better than corn chips	Is hungry right now	Likes hot dogs better than hamburgers
Doesn't like pizza	Likes chocolate milk better than plain milk	Doesn't like peanut butter and jelly together	Free space
Doesn't like chocolate	Likes yogurt	Likes ketchup and mustard on a hamburger	Doesn't like to eat fish

Session 6

Praying the Psalms

Scripture

"When you pray, go away by yourself, shut the door behind you, and pray to your Father secretly. Then your Father, who knows all secrets, will reward you." Matthew 6:6

Goal

Learn how to turn the psalms into prayers.

INTRODUCTION

As the students arrive, give each one a copy of the Psalm in Code handout (page 52). Tell the students to follow the instructions on the page to decode the psalm.

Answer: Open my eyes to see wonderful things in your teachings.

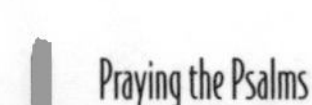

DISCOVERY RALLY

Gather the students together in a large group.

WHAT'S THE GOOD WORD?

Choose a student to read the Scripture for today.

THE CHALLENGE

Ask: **What was the psalm that you decoded? Is it a psalm that you could pray? Many of the psalms are prayers. Other psalms are not prayers, but they can be turned into prayers.** Tell the students that they will learn how to use psalms as prayers in their Discovery Centers today.

PRAYER

DISCOVERY CENTERS

1. SCULPTOR AND STATUE

MATERIALS
copies of Prayer Verses From Psalm 119 handout (page 53)

Before the session, make one copy of the handout for each student. Make one extra copy and cut apart the verses.

DO: Divide the students into pairs. Ask them to choose one person to be the sculptor and the other to be the statue. Ask the statues to stand in front of the sculptors. Give each sculptor a different psalm verse that you copied and cut out. Have each sculptor read the verse and move her statue into a position that expresses that verse. Remind the statues to be still and allow the sculptors to move them into position. If you have a camera, take pictures of the statues and their sculptors. Then let the sculptors take turns reading their verses aloud as they stand in front of their statues. Ask both statues and sculptors to be seated.

DISCUSS: **Most of what we communicate to each other is communicated by our facial expressions and our body language. These things communicate more than our words do. Our tone of voice also communicates more than our words. Do you think our body language and facial expressions communicate to God? Does our**

tone of voice communicate to God? Tell the students that the verses they read as they sculpted were from a long prayer psalm.

DO: Give each student a copy of the Prayer Verses From Psalm 119 page. Read the verses on the page together as a prayer.

2. CLAY REBUS

MATERIALS
prepared index cards, modeling clay of different colors, light-colored construction paper, markers

Before the session, write these paraphrased verses of Psalm 121 on different index cards as follows. Use a different color of ink or crayon for the words that are *italicized.*

Card 1. I lift up my eyes to the *hills.*
Card 2. Where does my help come from?
My help comes from the Lord,
The Maker of *heaven* and *earth.*
Card 3. He will not let your *foot* slip.
Card 4. He who watches over you will not *sleep.*
Card 5. The Lord watches over you.
The Lord is your shade at your right *hand.*
Card 6. The *sun* will not harm you by day.
Card 7. The *moon* will not harm you by night.
Card 8. The Lord will *guard* you from all dangers.
He will guard your life.
Card 9. The Lord will *guard* you as you come and go,
both now and forever.

DO: Give each student a piece of construction paper, a marker, modeling clay, and a prepared index card. Tell the students to write the words of the verse on the paper, except for the word that is the different color. For that word, the student is to use the clay to make that image or an image that represents that word. Ask the students to place their clay figures on the paper at the place where that word would go. (Suggest that the student who has the words *heaven* and *earth* make clouds and rocks or land forms as their figures. The student who has *sleeps* may model closed eyes with the clay. And the students who have the word *guard* may make a shield or sword or both.) When the students have finished making their figures, ask them to read their verses aloud in turn in order to say the full psalm.

DISCUSS: **Is this psalm a prayer?** Go back to each student in turn, helping the students turn each verse into something spoken to God. It will sound something like the following. (The italicized words are those that were changed to make this paraphrased psalm a prayer.)

I lift up my eyes to the hills.
Where does my help come from?
My help comes from *you,*
the Maker of heaven and earth.
You will not let *my* foot slip.
You who watch over me will not sleep.
You watch over me.
You are *my* shade at *my* right hand.
The sun will not harm *me* by day.
The moon will not harm *me* by night.
You will guard *me* from all dangers.
You will guard *my* life.
You will guard *me* as *I* come and go,
both now and forever.

If you have time, say Psalm 121 together again as a prayer.

3. THE TWENTY-THIRD PSALM

MATERIALS
white paper, tape, markers, drinking straws; yarn, narrow ribbon, or string cut into 3-foot lengths

DO: Give each student two sheets of paper. Ask the students to lay the papers with short ends together. Tape these ends together to make a long strip of paper. Turn the paper so that the short ends are at the top and bottom. Then give each student a Bible, and ask the students to turn to Psalm 23. Tell them that parts of this psalm sound like David talking to God. Other parts don't. Tell the students that you will help them write this psalm on their papers as a prayer.

Ask the students how they would change the first verse so that it's talking to God. Ask the students to write, "You are my shepherd. I shall lack nothing." Ask how to change the second verse into a prayer. Then ask them to write, "You make me lie down in green pastures, you lead me beside still waters." Continue through the psalm in this way, helping students write the psalm on the length of their pages. Tape a third piece of paper onto the page if they run out of room. Their psalms should read something like this:

You are my shepherd, I shall lack nothing.
You make me lie down in green pastures.
You lead me beside quiet waters.
You restore my soul.
You guide me in paths of righteousness
for your name's sake.
Even though I walk
through the valley of the shadow of death,
I will fear no evil, for you are with me.
Your rod and staff, they comfort me.
You prepare a table before me
in the presence of my enemies.
You anoint my head with oil, my cup overflows.
Surely goodness and love will follow me
all the days of my life,
and I will dwell in your house, O Lord, forever.

When the students finish writing the psalm, give each of them two drinking straws. Ask them to tape one straw along the top edge of the page and one along the lower edge of the page. Then give them each a length of yarn, narrow ribbon, or string. Have them thread this through the straw at the top of the paper as shown, and tie it so that it makes a loop for hanging the psalm on the student's door or wall at home.

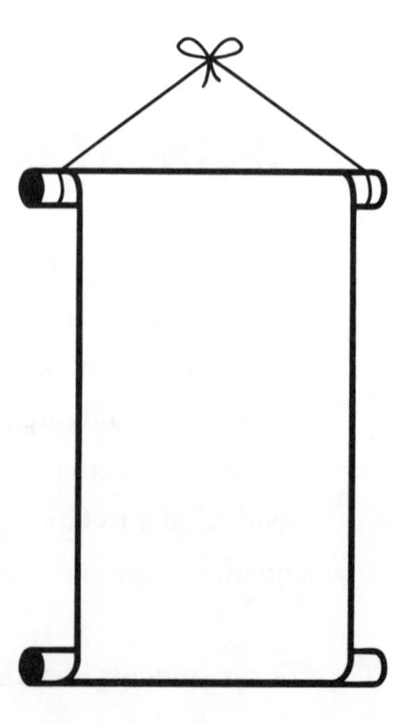

DISCUSS: Ask the students what made this psalm into a prayer. Ask them how they could make other psalms into prayers.

DISCOVERERS' DEBRIEFING

If you have time to review, gather as a large group and discuss your young discoverers' findings. Ask the following questions:

- **What is the most interesting thing you discovered today?**
- **What did you learn today that you didn't know before?**
- **Many psalms, like Psalm 119, are prayers already. Can we use those psalms as prayers of our own? If so, how? If not, why not?**
- **Many psalms are not prayers. How can we turn them into prayers?**

Review the Scripture for today.

Pray Psalm 121. (Each student should have a page of this psalm from Discovery Center #2.)

Psalm In Code

Figure out the words to this prayer psalm.

O +   M +      2

_ _ _ _   _ _   _ _ _ _ _   _ _

1 +   + ful

_ _ _   _ _ _ _ _ _ _ _ _

th +   -r   N   u + R

_ _ _ _ _ _   _ _   _ _ _ _

_ _ _ _ _ _ _ _ _ . from PSALM 119:18, ICB

PRAYER VERSES FROM PSALM 119

- "I rejoice in following your statutes as one rejoices in great riches."
  Psalm 119:14, NIV

- "I think about your orders and study your ways."
  Psalm 119:15, ICB

- "I am sad and tired. Make me strong again as you have promised."
  Psalm 119:28, ICB

- "I run in the path of your commands, for you have set my heart free."
  Psalm 119:32, NIV

- "How sweet are your words to my taste, sweeter than honey to my mouth!"
  Psalm 119:103, NIV

- "I shake in fear of you. I fear your laws."
  Psalm 119:120, ICB

- "I open my mouth and pant, longing for your commands."
  Psalm 119:131, NIV

- "Streams of tears flow from my eyes, for your law is not obeyed."
  Psalm 119:136, NIV

Session 7

Praying God's Word

Scripture

"This is the confidence we have in approaching God: that if we ask anything according to his will, he hears us. And if we know that he hears us—whatever we ask—we know that we have what we asked of him." 1 John 5:14, 15

Goal

Learn how to pray according to God's will by praying Scriptures, and explore some of the answers that God gives when we pray.

INTRODUCTION

As the students arrive, give each one a copy of the Morse Code handout (page 58). Or before the session, prepare a poster board with "God loves you" written in Morse code and place it where all the students can see it. Give the students paper and pencils and ask them to write their names in Morse code and then tap their names in this code. If they have time, tell them to write "God hears us" in Morse code and then tap it out. If you bring flashlights, they can practice flashing the code.

DISCOVERY RALLY

Gather the students together in a large group.

WHAT'S THE GOOD WORD?

Choose a student to read the Scripture for today.

THE CHALLENGE

Ask the students to tap the pointer finger and middle finger of their right hands on their left palms in the Morse code rhythm for the word *God*. Ask: **What would you expect in return if you were sending a Morse code signal to someone? Yes, you would probably expect an answer. When you talk to a friend, you don't expect your friend to ignore you. You expect your friend to respond and talk to you.** Tell the students that today in their Discovery Centers they will learn about some ways God answers prayer.

PRAYER

DISCOVERY CENTERS

1. A PUZZLE PRAYER

Before the session, cut apart the Treasure Verses. Glue or tape each verse to an index card.

MATERIALS
prepared index cards, copies of the Jigsaw Puzzle handout (page 59) and the Treasure Verses handout (page 60), envelopes

DO: Give each student an envelope and a copy of the Jigsaw Puzzle handout. Turn the Treasure Verse cards upside down and let each student choose one. Ask each student to reads his verse aloud for the group. After a student reads his verse, ask: **How can we turn this verse into a prayer?** (See suggestions on page 61.) When the group has finished turning each verse into a prayer, each student should copy his verse onto the jigsaw puzzle page. Ask the students to cut out their jigsaw puzzle pieces, put the pieces into their envelopes, and write their names on their envelopes. If you have time, have the students exchange envelopes and try to put together someone else's puzzle.

DISCUSS: Ask a student to read the Scripture for today. **How do we know if we are praying "according to God's will"? Where do we find out what God's will is? Since we know the Bible tells us God's will, we can know we are praying according to God's will by praying the Scriptures. If we are praying according to God's will, we know we will receive what we pray for** (1 John 5:14, 15). Challenge each student to pray the Treasure Verse that is written on her puzzle page this week.

2. A SWEET MOSAIC

MATERIALS
construction paper, markers, glue, colorful dry cereal, bowls

DO: Give each student a piece of construction paper. Ask the students to write, "Seek first God's kingdom" (Matthew 6:33) on the paper in large block letters. Pour colorful sweet dry cereal into bowls and let the students glue the colorful shapes onto the letters to make a mosaic.

DISCUSS: **Have you ever asked for something sweet to eat, but the person in charge said no, because it was too close to dinnertime? Have you ever told a younger brother no because what he wanted was dangerous or bad for him? Have you ever done something you wanted to do, or got something you wanted, and it turned out to be bad for you?** If so, ask students to explain what that situation was. **Sometimes we wish someone had told us no. Why might God not give us what we ask for? He knows what's best. Sometimes what we ask for is not good for us.**

3. SEARCHING FOR THE RIGHT WORDS

MATERIALS
copies of A Word Search handout (page 62), pencils

DO: Give each student a copy of A Word Search handout. Ask one of the students to read Matthew 7:7, "Seek and you will find." Tell the students to follow the directions on the page to find the words. As students ask for help, give help. Don't help if you are not asked. ("Ask and you will receive.")

DISCUSS: Ask if the students who asked for help found it easier to do the word search. **Life is easier if we ask for God's help. Does God help with school work?** Ask a student to read Daniel 1:17 ("To these four young men God gave knowledge and understanding of all kinds of literature and learning.") **How could you turn this into a prayer?** ("God, give me knowledge and understanding of all kinds of literature and learning.") **Does God help us with Bible study?** Ask a student to read Luke 24:45, NIV ("Then he [Jesus] opened their minds so they could understand the Scriptures.") **How could this verse be turned into a prayer?** ("Jesus, open my mind so I can understand the Scriptures.")

DISCOVERERS' DEBRIEFING

If you have time to review, gather as a large group and discuss your young discoverers' findings. Ask the following questions:

- **What is the most interesting thing you discovered today?**
- **What did you learn today that you didn't know before?**
- **How can we know that we are praying according to God's will?**
- **How can we turn Scriptures into prayers?**
- **Why might God say no in answer to a prayer?**
- **What Scripture can we pray to get help with school work?**
- **What Scripture can we pray to get help with Bible study?**

Review the Scripture for today.

Pray Daniel 1:17 and Luke 24:45. Ask God to help us know his will better.

MORSE CODE

There are many ways we communicate with people. How many ways can you think of? Long ago, Morse code was invented. You can tap it or flash it with light. Using the Morse code alphabet, write out the signal for "GOD LOVES YOU."

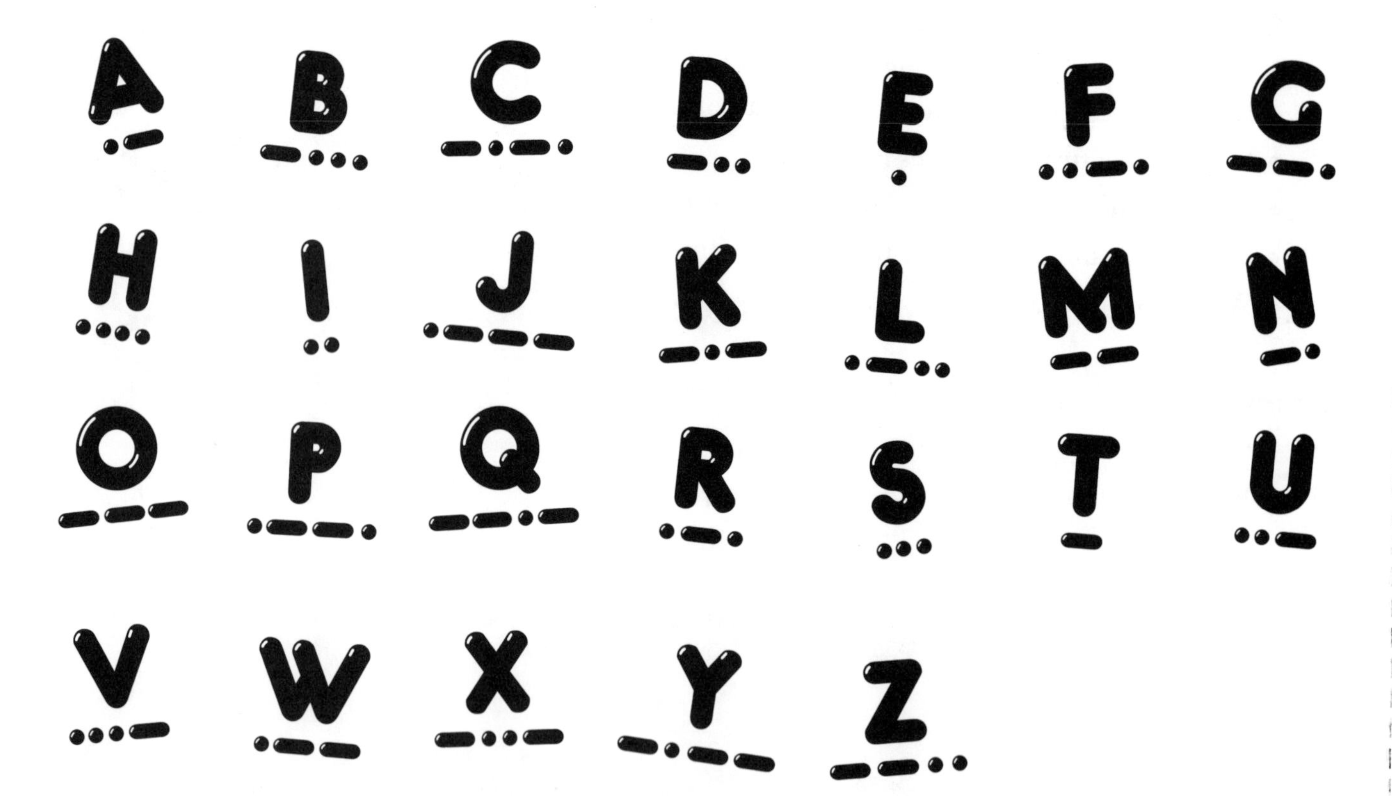

Jigsaw Puzzle

TREASURE VERSES

"Let us be alert and self-controlled." 1 Thessalonians 5:6

"Be on your guard; stand firm in the faith; be men of courage; be strong." 1 Corinthians 16:13

"May the God of peace . . . equip you with everything good for doing his will, and may he work in us what is pleasing to him." Hebrews 13:20, 21

"Make sure that nobody pays back wrong for wrong, but always try to be kind to each other and to everyone else." 1 Thessalonians 5:15

"Do not store up for yourselves treasures on earth, where moth and rust destroy, and where thieves break in and steal. But store up for yourselves treasures in heaven, where moth and rust do not destroy, and where thieves do not break in and steal." Matthew 6:19, 20

"Everyone should be quick to listen, slow to speak and slow to become angry." James 1:19

"Dear friend, do not imitate what is evil but what is good." 3 John 11

"Command them to do good, to be rich in good deeds, and to be generous and willing to share." 1 Timothy 6:18

"Let us not become weary in doing good, for at the proper time we will reap a harvest if we do not give up." Galatians 6:9

"I want you to be wise about what is good, and innocent about what is evil." Romans 16:19

Turning Treasure Verses Into Prayers

"Dear Lord, help me be alert and self-controlled." 1 Thessalonians 5:6

"Dear Lord, help me to be on my guard. I want to stand firm in my faith. Give me courage and help me to be strong." 1 Corinthians 16:13

"Dear Lord, equip me with everything good for doing your will, and work in me what is pleasing to you." Hebrews 13:20, 21

"Dear Lord, help me not to pay back wrong for wrong. Help me to be kind to others." 1 Thessalonians 5:15

"Dear Lord, I'm not going to store up treasures here on earth where moth and rust destroy, and where thieves break in and steal. Help me to store up treasures in heaven instead, because I know that in heaven moth and rust don't destroy, and thieves cannot break in and steal." Matthew 6:19, 20

"Dear Lord, help me to be quick to listen. Help me to be slow to speak. Help me to be slow to become angry." James 1:19

"Dear Lord, help me not to imitate what is evil but to imitate what is good." 3 John 11

"Dear Lord, help me to be rich in good deeds. Help me to be generous and willing to share." 1 Timothy 6:18

"Dear Lord, help me to not become weary in doing good. I know that at the right time I will reap a harvest if I don't give up." Galatians 6:9

"Dear Lord, help me to be wise about what's good and innocent about what's evil." Romans 16:19

A WORD SEARCH

The Clues: **God listens to your prayers no matter what happens. In the blanks on the right, put the opposite of the word on the left. The first word is done for you.**

God hears your prayers whether you are

rich	or	p o o r
sick	or	_ _ l _
fat	or	_ h _ _
unhurt	or	_ _ r _
peaceful	or	a _ g _ _
enemy	or	f _ _ _ _ _
tall	or	_ h _ _ _
little	or	_ i _
interested	or	b _ r _ _
serious	or	s _ l _ y
last	or	_ i _ _ _
outgoing	or	_ h _
down	or	_ _
sad	or	_ _ _ _ y
afraid	or	_ o _ _

The Word Search: **Each word you wrote in the blanks above will also be in a row or column in the puzzle below. Find each word and circle it.**

J	H	A	P	P	Y	S	B
O	U	S	H	O	R	T	O
F	R	I	E	N	D	W	R
I	T	L	T	U	P	E	E
R	O	L	H	B	O	L	D
S	H	Y	I	I	O	L	A
T	Z	A	N	G	R	Y	P

Prayer Journals

Scripture

"Jesus told his disciples a parable to show them that they should always pray and not give up." Luke 18:1

Goal

Learn how to journal our prayers. Explore why God might answer "no" or "wait." Learn that God wants us to keep on praying as we wait for his answers.

INTRODUCTION

As students arrive, give them copies of the Alphabet Soup Game handout (page 69). Ask them to follow the directions to figure out the letters described by each clue. (The answers are J, I, B, T, P, C, Y, E, N, U.)

DISCOVERY RALLY

Gather the students together in a large group.

WHAT'S THE GOOD WORD?

Choose a student to read the Scripture for today.

THE CHALLENGE

Read aloud the Alphabet Soup Game clues from the introductory activity, and let the students tell you the letter that is described by each clue. Ask: **Do you have a favorite letter of the alphabet?** If any of them has a favorite, let him tell what that letter is and why it is a favorite. **Of course, we would not need letters if we didn't read or write. What forms of communication require writing?** (Letters, e-mail, newspapers, magazines.) **What forms of communication don't require writing?** (Radio, television, video.) **Prayer is a form of communication that doesn't require writing. But there is a way to write what we're praying about. Writing what we pray about helps us watch and wait for God's answers.** Tell the students that today in their Discovery Centers they will learn about journaling their prayers and God's answers.

PRAYER

DISCOVERY CENTERS

1. PRAYER JOURNALS

MATERIALS
loose-leaf folders, notebook paper, tabbed divider pages, markers

DO: Give each student a folder, paper, and three tabbed divider pages. Ask the students to label the divider pages as follows:

- On the tab of one divider page write, "I asked."
  On the front of that same divider write, "What I Asked God."
- On the tab of the second divider, write, "God answered." On the front of that same divider, write, "How God Answered."
- On the tab of the third divider, write, "God Taught Me." On the front of that same divider, write, "What God Taught Me."

Ask the students to put their notebook paper and the dividers into the folder. (If this is your third group, they will have already filled out one page for each section. They may place these pages in the appropriate sections of their folders.) Ask the students to write "Prayer Journal" on the front of the folder and decorate it using markers, crayons, or stickers. Ask the students to take their journals with them to the next Discovery Center.

DISCUSS: What do you think should be recorded in the section marked "I asked"? What should you record in the section marked "God answered"? What should you record in the section marked "God taught me"? Tell of a prayer that you or someone else prayed that God answered "yes." Tell of a prayer that you or someone else prayed that God answered "no." Tell of a prayer that you or someone else prayed and are still praying and waiting for an answer. Why might God answer "no" or "wait"? (See the additional information at the end of the lesson for suggestions about this if you need help.)

2. OUR PRAYERS

MATERIALS
notebook paper or prayer journals created in Discovery Center #1, pens or pencils

DO: *If this is your first group,* give each student three pages of notebook paper. As a title on the first page, have them write, "I Asked." Have students write the title of the second page, "God Answered," and the third page, "God Taught Me." *If this is your second or third group,* ask them to open to the first section of their folders ("I Asked").

Ask the students to think of things they need to pray about, or things they are already including in their prayers. Ask them to write today's date on the first line available in the "I Asked" section (or page). Have them list things they are praying about or need to pray about. Suggest that the students write some of the things that other students list so that these become things they are praying about for each other.

Ask the students to turn to the section (or page) entitled "God Answered." Tell them that when God answers one of the prayers listed in the "I Asked" section, they are to write God's answer in this section.

Ask the students to turn to the section (or page) entitled "God Taught Me." Tell them that in this section they will write things God teaches them as they pray and he answers.

DISCUSS: **Why does God want us to pray? What possible answers could God give to our prayers? What might God teach us through prayer?** (Patience, the importance of coming to him, trust, his wisdom and good timing.) **Why might God answer "no" to a prayer? Why might he answer "wait?"** (See the additional information at the end of this lesson for suggestions on why God might answer "no.")

If you have time, ask a student to read Colossians 4:12. **What do you think it means to "wrestle in prayer"? Why would Epaphras "wrestle in prayer"?**

3. THE "STICK-WITH-IT" STICK

MATERIALS
large craft stick or tongue depressor, markers, modeling clay

DO: Ask a student to read the parable of the persistent widow, Luke 18:1-8. Then give each student a craft stick. Ask the students to write "Stick with it" on one side of their sticks with a marker. Then they may decorate the sticks with marker designs. When they are finished, give each student a piece of clay to make a base in which to stand the stick. Send these home as reminders to keep on praying.

DISCUSS: **Why do you think Jesus told the parable of the persistent widow? Why should we have to pray anything more than once? Does God not hear us the first time? What can God teach us when we pray again and again for the same thing?** (Persistence, patience, trust, dependence on God, contentment or thankfulness for what God has given us.)

Discoverers' Debriefing

DISCOVERER'S DEBRIEFING

If you have time to review, gather as a large group and discuss your young discoverers' findings. Ask the following questions:

- **What is the most interesting thing you discovered today?**
- **What did you learn today that you didn't know before?**
- **How can we journal our prayers?**

- **Why does God want us to keep on praying for some things?**
- **Why would God answer our prayer by saying "wait"?**
- **Why would God answer "no"?**

Review the Scripture for today.

Pray, thanking God for always hearing our prayers. Tell God that you trust him to always give the right answer because of his great wisdom. Ask him to continue to teach us to pray.

ADDITIONAL BIBLE BACKGROUND

Why would God answer "no"?
This is related to the questions, "Why do bad things happen if I'm praying for them not to happen?" and "Why do we pray for some people to get well, and they don't?" and "Why do we pray for some people to live, but they die?"

1. We must realize that God is always our provider. He will give us all we need "for life and godliness" (2 Peter 1:3). In Matthew 6:33, Jesus tells us that if we seek God's kingdom and his righteousness first, God will give us the things we need. God is so much greater and wiser than we are, his view of what we need and our view of what we need are sometimes different. (See Isaiah 55:8, 9.)

2. God has already given us many things that we have not been thankful for. If we give to someone who never expresses thanks for what we give, we are very likely to wonder whether we should give them anything else. To make matters worse, we not only forget to thank God for all he gives us, but we complain about things and worry about things, not trusting God to take care of us and provide all that we need. Perhaps we need to stop complaining and start trusting and be thankful.

3. Sometimes we ask for things we don't need, or for things that would be bad for us. Remind students of last week's discussion about asking for candy when it's too close to dinnertime. Sometimes even our parents say no when what we ask for would be bad for us.

4. Read James 4:3. "When you ask, you do not receive, because you ask with wrong motives, that you may spend what you get on your pleasures."

5. God uses hard times in our lives to train us and grow us up mentally, emotionally, and spiritually. Read Hebrews 12:7. "Endure hardship as discipline; God is treating you as sons." Discipline is training, not punishment. Punishment has to do with past sins. Jesus was punished for our sins. Discipline has to do with the future. God is training us for the future. Read also James 1:2-4.

Ultimately, we must rely on God's sovereign wisdom and timing to answer all our prayers perfectly. We don't always understand. God's ways are mysteries to us, because he is God. Remember what Shadrach, Meshach, and Abednego said, "The God we serve is able to save us . . . and he will rescue us. . . . But even if he does not . . . we will not serve your gods" (Daniel 3:17, 18). They wanted to be saved from the fiery furnace. But they knew that God is God, and that no matter what his answer was, it would be right.

ALPHABET SOUP GAME

WRITE THE LETTER OF THE ALPHABET THAT ANSWERS EACH CLUE.

WHAT LETTER IS

A BIRD? ____________________

PART OF YOUR HEAD? ____________________

AN INSECT? ____________________

A DRINK? ____________________

A VEGETABLE? ____________________

A BODY OF WATER? ____________________

A QUESTION? ____________________

SOMETHING A SCARED PERSON MIGHT SAY WHEN HE SEES A MOUSE?

____

THE OPPOSITE OF "OUT"? ____________________

A MOTHER SHEEP? ____________________

Session 9

Fighting With Prayer

Scripture

"Take the helmet of salvation and the sword of the Spirit, which is the word of God. And pray in the Spirit on all occasions with all kinds of prayers and requests."
Ephesians 6:17, 18

Goal

Learn how to use prayer as a spiritual weapon.

INTRODUCTION

As students arrive, give each student a 1-by-2-foot length of butcher paper or newsprint and a small sponge. Pour water-based paint into the bottoms of enough paper plates for several groups of students to share. Use green paint in half of the plates and brown paint in the other plates. Ask students to write their names on the backs of their pieces of paper. Then they should make a camouflage pattern on the front of the paper by pressing their sponges into the paint on the plates and then onto the paper, making brown and green patches. Bring a hair dryer, and gently blow warm air on these to speed the drying of the paint. You will use them for Discovery Center #3.

DISCOVERY RALLY

Gather the students together in a large group.

WHAT'S THE GOOD WORD?

Choose a student to read the Scripture for the day.

THE CHALLENGE

Ask a student to read Matthew 5:44. **What does this verse mean? Have you ever heard of fighting with prayer (or "spiritual warfare")? What does that mean? If we are fighting, who is the enemy we are fighting against?** Tell them that today in their Discovery Centers they will learn more about using prayer as a weapon to fight the enemy.

PRAYER

DISCOVERY CENTERS

1. NEWS PRAYERS

MATERIALS

stories clipped from newspapers and newsmagazines

DO: Give each student a news story to read silently. Then have them take turns briefly telling the group about the article they read. After each student tells about her article, ask how she could pray for the subject of that article. Then ask that student to say a brief prayer about that subject. If the student is too shy or doesn't know what to say, you may say the prayer and model this kind of prayer. For example, if the article is about the President, pray for the President. If the article is about another nation, pray for God's Word to spread to that nation. If the article is about a disaster somewhere, pray for God to heal and comfort. Ask God to defeat the enemy's plans and to turn this event into something that will bring God glory.

DISCUSS: **What would you say to God about your article? Is there a Scripture that you could pray about the subject? Someone once said that our prayers can go places where even missionaries can't go. Where are your prayers reaching right now? Who is our spiritual enemy?** (See Mark 4:15; John 8:44; 1 Peter 5:8, 9;

Revelation 12:9.) **Our prayers can fight the enemy in places where physical armies can't go.**

If you have time, read 2 Kings 6:15-17. Then read Psalm 68:17. Ask the students what these passages tell us about God and his ability to fight the enemy.

2. CARROT PRINT SWORDS

MATERIALS
carrots cut in half lengthwise, colored construction paper, paper plates, silver, gray, gold, or white paint

DO: Give each student a piece of construction paper and a carrot half. Pour paint into the bottom of some paper plates. Ask the students to carefully press the flat side of the carrot half into the paint and then onto their paper. (This creates a shape that looks like a sword blade.) Then ask the students to draw a hilt (handle) of any design on their sword. Have them write across the bottom of the paper, "Take the sword of the Spirit, which is the word of God." (Verse is taken from Ephesians 6:17.) As a group, try turning Ephesians 6:14-17 into a prayer.

DISCUSS: **Why would God call his word "the sword of the Spirit"?** Ask a student to read Matthew 4:1-10. **How did Jesus fight temptation in this passage?** (Jesus used the sword of the Spirit, the Word of God, to fight temptation.) **How can we turn Scriptures into prayers? For example, if we are tempted to be afraid, we can use the sword of the Spirit to fight that temptation by saying, "I will not be afraid, because it is written, 'In God I trust; I will not be afraid' (Psalm 56:4)." Or to fight pride, we can say, "I will not be prideful, because it is written, 'God opposes the proud but gives grace to the humble' (James 4:6)."**

If you have time, let students suggest temptations that they fight, and look up Scriptures in a concordance to help them fight those specific temptations.

3. CAMOUFLAGE BIBLE COVERS

MATERIALS
camouflage paper from the introductory activity, hair dryer, scissors, tape

DO: Use the hair dryer to finish drying any of the camouflage paper that is still damp. Then help the students cover their Bibles or the classroom Bibles as shown in the diagram.

DISCUSS: Why does God call his Word the "sword of the Spirit"? How can we use Scriptures as prayers? Help students turn Ephesians 6:14-17 into a prayer. **"Dear Lord, help me stand firm in my faith. Secure the belt of truth around my waist. Secure the breastplate of righteousness in place across my chest. Make my feet ready with the good news of peace. Put the shield of faith in one of my hands and your sword of the Spirit in the other."**

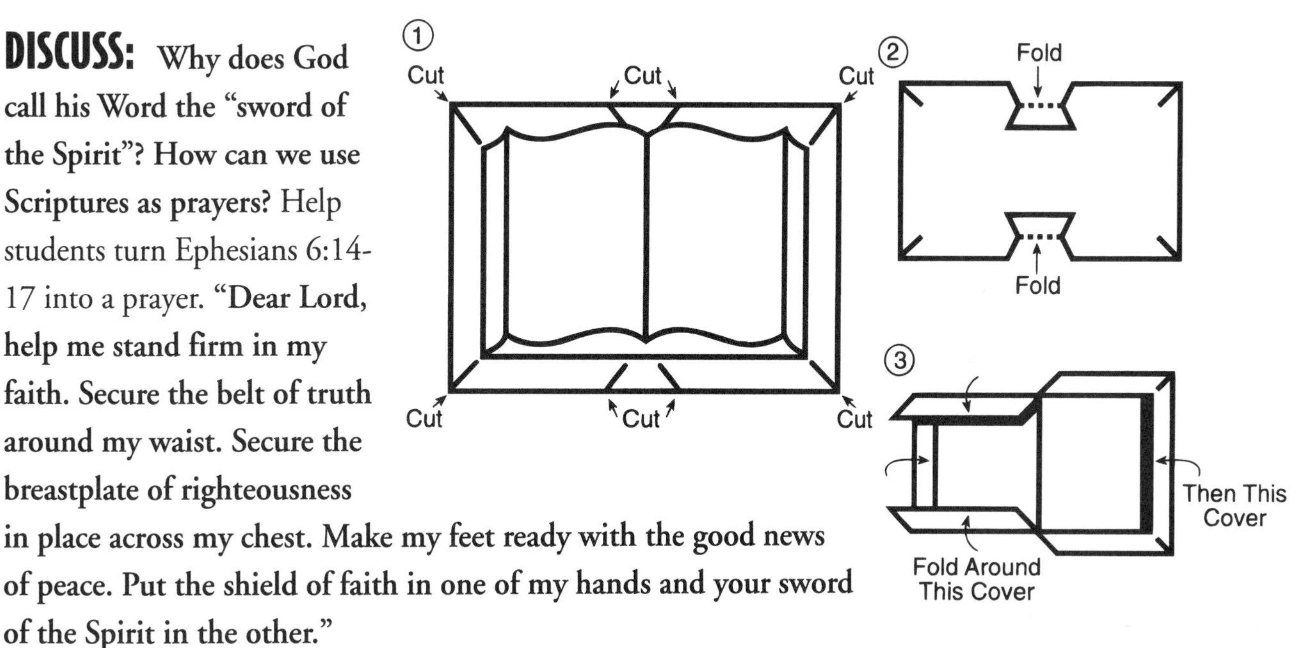

DISCOVERERS' DEBRIEFING

If you have time to review, gather as a large group and discuss your young discoverers' findings. Ask the following questions:

- **What is the most interesting thing you discovered today?**
- **What did you learn today that you didn't know before?**
- **What is the sword of the Spirit?**
- **How can we use the sword of the Spirit?**
- **Who is our enemy?**
- **Do we need to fight the enemy? Why or why not?**
- **How can we fight temptation?**

Review the Scripture for today.

Pray, asking God to train you to fight using prayer and the sword of the Spirit.

Session 10

Bridge Prayers: Intercession

Scripture

"God knows how often I pray for you. Day and night I bring you and your needs in prayer to God." Romans 1:9, NLT

Goal

Learn that intercession is prayer for other people and situations.
Learn that God wants us to intercede for others.

INTRODUCTION

As students arrive, send each student to one of three tables on which you have placed a large package of miniature marshmallows and two boxes of toothpicks. Tell the students that they are to work together to build a bridge at their table. Tell them they can use their imaginations and build it any way they want as long as they work together, letting everyone share ideas and help with the building of the bridge. If one group finishes before another, challenge them to set two chairs one foot apart and build a bridge between them using the marshmallows and toothpicks.

DISCOVERY RALLY

Gather students together in a large group.

WHAT'S THE GOOD WORD?

Choose a student to read the Scripture for today.

THE CHALLENGE

Point out the bridges that were built in the introductory activity. Let the group that built each bridge raise their hands as you point to their bridge. Ask: **Can you describe some bridges you have seen? How are they alike? How are they different?** Tell them that today in their Discovery Groups they will find out about "bridge prayers."

PRAYER

DISCOVERY CENTERS

1. THE GO-BETWEEN

MATERIALS
paper, tape

DO: Roll a small piece of plain paper into a tube and tape it closed. Gather your group together on the floor. Seat one student in a chair in front of the group with his back to the group. Designate another student to be the king. The king stands or kneels behind the students seated on the floor. Place the rolled paper on the floor behind the student in the chair. Pretend that the student in the chair has written on this paper a list of some things he needs. Then while the student in the chair is not looking, quietly point to a student sitting on the floor. This student is the Go-Between. She must sneak up very quietly behind the chair, pick up the paper, and take it to the king. When the Go-Between has returned to her seat on the floor, the group should say together, "Your list is gone. Who took your list?" Then the student in the chair stands up and faces the group. This student has two guesses to find out which student was the Go-Between. If the student guesses correctly, then the Go-Between gets to sit in the chair and the student from the chair becomes the king. The old king sits on the floor with the rest of the students. But if the student in the chair does not guess correctly, then he stays in the chair, the paper is placed behind him, and another Go-Between is chosen.

DISCUSS: **The word *intercession* means "going between." What do we "go between" in prayer?** (We go between a person who has a need and God. Or we go between a situation and God. Or between our nation and God. We intercede. We pray for someone else or for another situation. It's like taking the message to the king in the game. We are taking a prayer request to the King in heaven.) **Who are some people we can intercede for today? What are some situations we can intercede for today?**

2. CROSSING THE GAP

MATERIALS
large metal paper clip, bit of modeling clay, balloon, and a piece of wool cloth (or a wool sweater, jacket, scarf, or socks)

DO: Ask a student to stand the paper clip upright with the clay as its base. Let the students take turns rubbing the balloon across the wool, then holding the balloon close to the top of the paper clip. Tell the students to listen carefully as the balloon is held near the clip. (They should hear a faint snapping sound. This is because the balloon has picked up electrons from the wool, and when the balloon gets close to the paper clip, these electrons jump across the gap through the air to the paper clip, making a crackle or snap as they jump.) If it is a dry day, ask the students to comb through their hair to hear the electrons jumping back to their hair from the comb.

DISCUSS: **In this experiment something we could not see crossed the gap between the balloon and the paper clip. Sometimes there seems to be a gap between people or nations or situations and God. Interceding is like crossing the gap between our nation and God, or a person and God, or a situation and God.** Ask a student to read Ezekiel 22:30. **God was looking for someone who would put him first and come to him praying for the people of the land.** Read Genesis 18:20-33. **For whom or what did Abraham intercede? What was God's answer? For whom can we intercede?** (Our nation, our President, our friends and family, missionaries, foreign nations and rulers.)

3. PRAYER BALL

MATERIALS
globe ball

DO: Before beginning your main activity, ask the students to write their names, phone numbers, and e-mail addresses (if they have them or know them) on a master list that you will keep. The person in charge of the introductory activity next week will need this list to prepare for next week's activity.

For your main activity, bring a ball that looks like a globe. (Some of these are inflatable, some are like soft pillows. If you can't find one, get a large, plain children's ball and draw continents on it with a permanent marker to make it look like a globe.) Form a circle with your group and toss the globe to a student. When the student catches it, ask the student to look at the globe where her right index finger is pointing. Then say a prayer for that nation. Point out that you are interceding for that nation. You are going between that nation and God. (If the student's right index finger is pointing to an area of ocean, look at where the left index finger is pointing, or pray for a country that the palm is touching.) Then the student holding the ball tosses it to another student. Locate the country this student's finger points to and pray for it.

DISCUSS: **What are some good things to ask God when we pray for countries? Do you know anyone who lives in this country? Have you heard anything in the news about this country? How can we intercede for our own country?**

Discoverers' Debriefing

DISCOVERERS' DEBRIEFING

If you have time to review, gather as a large group and discuss your young discoverers' findings. Ask the following questions:

- **What is the most interesting thing you discovered today?**
- **What did you learn today that you didn't know before?**
- **What is intercession?**
- **For what or whom does God want us to intercede? Why?**
- **How can you intercede for your family? for your friends?**
- **How can you intercede for our nation? for other nations?**

Review the Scripture for today.

Pray, interceding for your city, state, or nation.

NOTE: Youth With a Mission (YWAM) has an excellent prayer journal for students called *Tracking Your Walk*. It includes maps and information about other nations so that students can intercede for these nations. They also have "Daniel Prayer Groups" to involve students, teens, and families in intercession for the world.

For *Tracking Your Walk*, contact YWAM Publishing at P.O. Box 55787, Seattle, WA 98155 or on the web at http://www.ywampublishing.com or by calling 1-800-922-2143.

For more information on the Daniel Prayer Groups, contact

King's Kids/Daniel Prayer Groups
Stanely House 14, Stanely Crescent
Paisley PA2 9LF
Scotland, United Kingdom
e-mail: 100104.417@compuserve.com

Prayer Chains

Scripture

"Peter was kept in prison, but the church was earnestly praying to God for him." Acts 12:5

Goal

Learn that there is great power when we agree in prayer.

INTRODUCTION

Write or type the name and phone number of each student in your class in a list, skipping about five spaces between each name so that they can be cut into strips. This list will be a prayer chain for your class, so keep in mind that each student on the list will be telephoning or e-mailing the student listed immediately after him. Photocopy one list for each student in class using colored paper.

As students arrive, give each one a copy of the list. Ask the students to cut the list into strips with one student's name and phone number on each strip. If you have time, the students can ask each other to autograph the backs of the strips that have their names on it. Give each student an envelope in which to carry the strips or a paper clip to clip them together. They will need these strips for Discovery Center #1.

DISCOVERY RALLY

Gather the students together in a large group.

WHAT'S THE GOOD WORD?

Choose a student to read the Scripture for today.

THE CHALLENGE

Ask: **What are chains used for?** (Chains are used because of their strength.) **What is a prayer chain?** (A prayer chain is a group of people who agree to pray about the same thing. When prayer is needed for some reason, one person prays and calls the next person to tell them about the prayer need. The second person prays and calls a third person. The third person prays and calls a fourth person, and so on. In this way, many people can pray about the same thing.) Tell the students that in their Discovery Centers today they will learn more about prayer chains.

PRAYER

DISCOVERY CENTERS

1. MAKING THE PRAYER CHAIN

MATERIALS
strips from introductory activity, tape or staplers

DO: Ask the students to make paper chains using the strips they cut out in the introductory activity. Use a copy of the list of names to tell the students the order in which to link the paper chains. Call out the first name on the list. Ask the students to find the strip with that name on it and loop it into a circle with ends overlapping. Tape or staple the ends in place. Call out the second name on the list. Ask the students to loop the strip with that name through the first ring, overlap its ends, and tape or staple in place. Continue in this way, making a chain out of all the names. (If your class is unusually large, you may need to use half or even one-third the number of links in the chain as students in class.)

DISCUSS: **Take these chains home and hang them in a place where you can easily locate them if you need to call other students to pray for something. Look at the chain and find your name. Whom would you call if you wanted the class to pray about something?** (You would call the person who comes after your name in the chain.) **What happens if the last person in the chain wants prayer?** (She calls the first person in the chain. That person calls the next person, and so on.) **Who would be the person calling you with a prayer request?** (It would most likely be the person that comes just before you in the prayer chain.) **What if you call someone and they're not home or they're sick?** (Leave a message if you can, and go ahead and call the next person in the chain so that the prayer request does not stop with you.)

2. PRAYER REQUEST BOARDS

MATERIALS

half-sheets of poster board, 1/4-inch elastic cut into 3-foot lengths, duct tape, ruler, scissors, paper punch, colored 3-by-5-inch index cards

Before the session, prepare a stencil of a cross using a half-sheet of poster board. The cross should use the full length and width of the half-sheet as shown. Cut out the stencil.

DO: Give each student a half-sheet of poster board. Let the students take turns tracing around the stencil on their half-sheets. Then have the students cut out their crosses. Give each student a yard of elastic. Have them cut the elastic into lengths that are about 1 inch longer than the width of a section of the cross (so that about 1/2 inch of both ends of the elastic will wrap around the cross). Ask the students to tape or staple 1/2 inch of one end of each piece of elastic to the back of the cross and then wrap the elastic around the front of the cross. Remind the students to pull the elastic so that it is snug, but not too tight. Then have them tape the loose end to the back of the cross. Tell the students that it is OK to wrap the elastic diagonally across the front of the cross (see the illustrations). Ask the students to punch a hole in the center of the top of the cross so that it can be hung on a door or wall. Give each student a few index cards to slip behind the elastic on the front of the cross.

DISCUSS: **This is a prayer request board to hang somewhere in your house. You can write prayer requests on the index cards and slip them behind the elastic bands. These will be reminders of things you need to pray about. You might offer to let your families use this prayer request board at home. Where could you hang it? What are some other ways that we can be reminded to pray?** If students think of some prayer requests they have right then, let them write these on the cards. Then go ahead and pray about them.

3. MANY-HEADS-ARE-BETTER-THAN-ONE GAME

MATERIALS
several small items that will be familiar to students (drinking straw, string, crayon, sticky note pad, pencil, stick of gum, spoon, eraser, leaf, toothpick), tablecloth or sheet, paper, pen or pencil

DO: Arrange the items on the table before the students arrive and cover them with a tablecloth or sheet. Tell the students that they will have one minute to view the objects under the tablecloth. Tell them they must look silently. Take off the cloth for one minute, and then place the cloth back over the objects. Ask each student to list every item he can remember from the table. Then let one student be the recorder. Give this student a piece of paper and a pen or pencil. Let the other students take turns telling everything they remember seeing on the table. Ask the recorder to make a list of the items as they are mentioned. (If an item is mentioned by more than one student, the recorder lists it only the first time it's mentioned.) When everyone has had a turn, remove the cloth again and check the list. Did everyone together remember everything on the table?

DISCUSS: After everyone has had a chance to tell what he remembers seeing on the table, point out that some people remember one thing and some people remember another. **When we work together, we remember more. Two or more heads can be better than one. Does that apply to prayer? How could more prayers be better than one?** (When we pray with others, different people may pray for different parts of the situation because they see it from different viewpoints. For example, if someone is sick, one person may pray for healing of the sickness. Another may pray for strength and courage for the sick person. Another may pray for the doctors and the medicines. Another may pray for the sick person's family. Another may pray for the sick person's school work.)

If you have time, you may want to change what's on the table under the cloth and let the students play the game again.

DISCOVERERS' DEBRIEFING

If you have time to review, gather as a large group and discuss your young discoverers' findings. Ask the following questions:

- **What is the most interesting thing you discovered today?**
- **What did you learn today that you didn't know before?**
- **What is a prayer chain?**
- **Why are prayer chains good?**
- **When many people are praying for something, God hears lots of prayers about it. Does that mean God doesn't pay as much attention when just one person is praying for something?**

Review the Scripture for today.

If you have time, you may take prayer requests or review the prayer requests that were mentioned in Discovery Group #2. Pray about the requests the students had, and thank God for hearing each of our individual prayers as well as the prayers we all pray together.

Session 12

Our Prayer Friends: Jesus and the Holy Spirit

Scripture

"We do not know how to pray as we should. But the Spirit himself speaks to God for us, even begs God for us. The Spirit speaks to God with deep feelings that words cannot explain."
Romans 8:26, ICB

"Christ Jesus, who died—more than that, who was raised to life—is at the right hand of God and is also interceding for us."
Romans 8:34, NIV

Goal

Learn that Jesus and the Holy Spirit speak to God on our behalf.

INTRODUCTION

From newspapers, magazines, product boxes and labels, clip logos and emblems that represent commonly recognized brand names, sports teams, and schools. Cover the company, school, sports team name with opaque tape, paint, or liquid correction fluid, leaving only the design of the logo.

As the students arrive, give each one a logo or emblem. You can pin the logos to their shirts if you want. Ask the students to guess each other's logos. You can give students more than one logo to make it more interesting.

DISCOVERY RALLY

Gather the students together in a large group.

WHAT'S THE GOOD WORD?

Choose a student to read the Scripture for today.

THE CHALLENGE

Hold up each logo from the introductory activity and let the students tell you together which team, brand, or school the logo represents. Ask: **What do people think when they see someone wearing a shirt or cap with a certain logo on it? How many of you play on a sports team? What is your team's logo or mascot? What is your school's logo or mascot? When you wear your school's logo or your school colors, you are telling everyone who sees you that you belong with that group. How do people know we belong to Jesus?** (Read John 13:35. "All men will know that you are my disciples, if you love one another.") **When we love each other, we pray for each other.** Ask the students about the Scriptures that were just read (Romans 8:26, 34). **According to those Scriptures, who talks to God about us?** Tell the students that today in their Discovery Centers, they will learn more about our very special intercessors.

PRAYER

DISCOVERY CENTERS

1. WHO KNOWS YOUR HEART?

MATERIALS
copies of The Holy Spirit handouts (pages 88, 89), pencils

DO: Read Romans 8:26, 27. Give each student a pencil and a copy of The Holy Spirit handouts. Help the students complete the two activities.

DISCUSS: **Have you ever had feelings that you couldn't put into words? Sometimes when we pray, we have deep feelings about things, but we don't know exactly what to say. When that happens, we can know that the Holy Spirit is**

talking to God for us, saying just the right thing. But that's not the only time he talks to God about us. When is the Holy Spirit with us? Read 1 Corinthians 6:19.

2. OUR BEST FRIEND

MATERIALS
copies of the Best Friends handout (page 90), markers or crayons

DO: Give each student a copy of the Best Friends handout. Tell them to look at the shapes and then the spaces between the shapes. Ask them to tell you what word is spelled by the space between the shapes. Then give each student a pencil. Tell the students to write their names in block capital letters in the lower half of the page. Then ask them to use a marker or crayon and color in the shapes between the letters of their name just as in the name JESUS at the top of the page. When the spaces have been colored in, they should erase the pencil marks.

DISCUSS: Read Romans 8:34. **What do you remember about intercession from Session 10? How does Jesus intercede for us?** Read Hebrews 4:14-16. **What does a priest do?** (A priest prays to God for people.) **So how is Jesus our priest?** (He talks to God about us.) **How do we come to God's "throne of grace"?** (We come to God in prayer.)

3. THE COURT OF LAW

MATERIALS
prepared index cards

Before the session, prepare several index cards by writing the name of a sin on each card (stealing, cheating, lying, speaking rudely, disobeying).

DO: Have the students act out a simple trial. Choose one student to be the judge. Seat the judge in front of the students, facing them. Choose one student to be the accused and one to be the prosecutor who will bring charges against the accused. Tell the accused that we are pretending that he really is guilty of the sin he's being accused of. Hold the index cards in your hand facing you. The accused draws one of the cards and hands it to the prosecutor. The prosecutor then tells the judge what the accused has done wrong. Tell the students they must always address the judge by saying, "Your Honor." The judge asks the accused, "Is this charge against you true?" The accused answers, "Yes, it's true."

Say: **The punishment for the crime would ordinarily be chosen at this time. But this trial is similar to what happens every day before God. And if we have accepted Jesus as our Savior, here is what happens.** Choose a student to represent Jesus. Ask this student to stand facing the judge, between the prosecutor and the accused. Tell the students that the accused has received Jesus as his Savior. So Jesus says to the judge, who is God, "I have already taken the punishment for this sin." Then instruct the judge to say, "The accused is not guilty."

Play several more rounds of this mock trial, keeping the same prosecutor, judge and student who represents Jesus. They say their same lines. But change the accused. Each time you do the trial, the accused draws a different card from your hand.

DISCUSS: **What is "Jesus" doing in this situation?** (He is speaking to God on behalf of the accused person.) **So Jesus is the one who intercedes or goes between. Who does Jesus go between? What is the result of Jesus going to God on our behalf?** (This is what we call being "justified." We are declared not guilty by God because of Jesus' death and resurrection.) Read Hebrews 4:14-16. **Because Jesus intercedes for us, we can have confidence when we come to God in prayer. What is confidence? What does it mean to come before God with confidence?**

DISCOVERERS' DEBRIEFING

If you have time to review, gather as a large group and discuss your young discoverers' findings. Ask the following questions:

- **What is the most interesting thing you discovered today?**
- **What did you learn that you didn't know before?**
- **Who are our heavenly intercessors?**
- **How does the Holy Spirit intercede for us?**
- **How does Jesus intercede for us?**
- **What does it mean to come to God's throne with confidence?**

Review the Scriptures for today.

Pray, thanking God for Jesus and the Holy Spirit who intercede for us. Thank God for allowing us to come to his throne with confidence.

THE HOLY SPIRIT

Who is the Holy Spirit?

Each letter in the words HOLY SPIRIT is numbered.
Put the letters in the blanks with the matching number.

H O L Y S P I R I T
1 2 3 4 5 6 7 8 9 10

C __ U N __ E __ __ __ (John 14:16, 26)
2 5 3 2 8

__ __ V __ N G WA __ E __ (John 7:38, 39)
3 7 9 10 8

G __ F __ __ F G __ D (Acts 8:19, 20)
7 10 2 2

SPIRIT OF __ __ U __ __ (John 14:17)
10 8 10 1

How long will the Counselor, the Holy Spirit, be with us? (John 14:16)
Draw lines following the clue moves.
You will find the answer to the question.

Clue Moves

1. B1 to D1
2. B1 to B2
3. C1 to C2
4. B3 to D3
5. B3 to B4
6. D3 to D4
7. B4 to D4
8. B5 to B6
9. B5 to D5
10. C5 to C6
11. C5 to D6
12. B6 to C6
13. B7 to B8
14. B7 to D7
15. C7 to C8
16. D7 to D8
17. B9 to D9½
18. D9½ to B10
19. B11 to B12
20. B11 to D11
21. C11 to C12
22. D11 to D12
23. B13 to B14
24. B13 to D13
25. C13 to C14
24. C13 to D14
25. B14 to C14

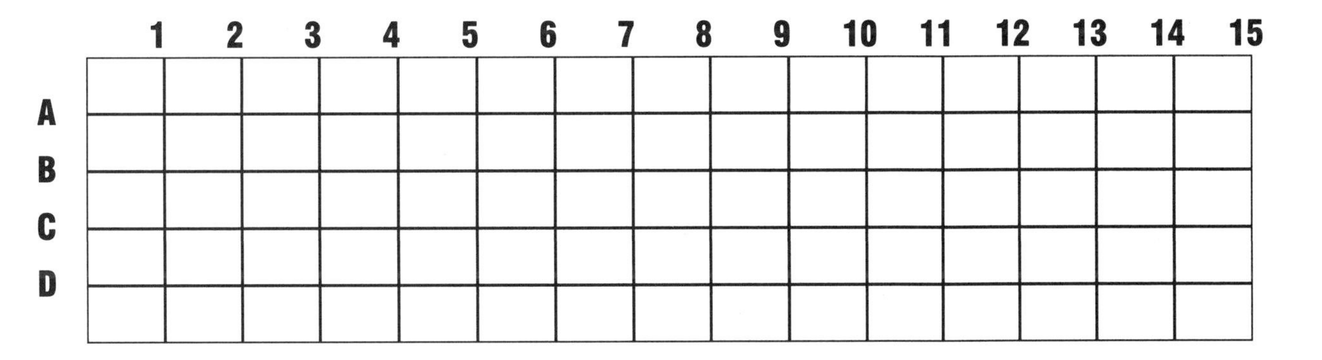

BEST FRIENDS

Session 13

My Personal Track

Scripture

"Do not worry about anything. But pray and ask God for everything you need. And when you pray, always give thanks. And God's peace will keep your hearts and minds in Christ Jesus." Philippians 4:6, 7, ICB

Goal

Pledge to pray and plan to pray.

INTRODUCTION

Bring some magnifying glasses and several ink pads containing washable ink. (As an option, you could pour a thin layer of washable paint into several paper plates.) As the students arrive, give each one a piece of manila paper. Tell each student to press both his left and right thumbs onto the ink pad and then "walk" them across his paper, making tracks like footprints. Have moist paper towels or hand wipes ready to clean off the students' thumbs when they have finished. Let them use the magnifying glasses to compare their thumbprints with those of other students to see how they are different.

DISCOVERY RALLY

Gather the students together in a large group.

WHAT'S THE GOOD WORD?

Choose a student to read the Scripture for today.

THE CHALLENGE

Show the track pictures made in the introductory activity. Ask: **How are the pictures different? Why? Each person is an individual, made by God to be unique. Just as our parents enjoy each of their children's unique personalities, so God also enjoys each of our different, unique personalities. After all, he made us this way! God enjoys the times when we talk to him, and he wants *us* to enjoy talking to him.** Tell the students that today in their Discovery Centers they will learn why and how to plan for time with God.

PRAYER

DISCOVERY CENTERS

1. PRAYING ON THE JOB

MATERIALS
prepared index cards, tape, poster board

Before the session, write one word of the following verse (and reference) on each of nine index cards: "Pray and ask God for everything you need" (Philippians 4:6). This is part of the Scripture for today. Also write the entire verse on a piece of poster board and display it where the group can see it. Before your first group arrives, tape the cards in mixed-up order underneath chairs. If you will have more than nine students in the group, the number of students greater than nine will sit in chairs with no cards underneath. If you will have fewer than nine students, you may tape more than one card under one or more chairs. Also, make yourself a master list of occupations, one to assign to each student (nurse, electrician, taxi driver, painter, lawyer, grocer).

DO: Ask the students to sit side by side with the chairs in a straight line or a semicircle. Decide which end of the line of chairs will be the beginning of the line. Assign each student an occupation from your master list. Then say something like, "I pray throughout the day, working at the hospital." Tell the students that the person who has been assigned the occupation of nurse must get up and run to the first chair. Ask the students from the first chair to the chair left vacant by the nurse to move down one seat so that the nurse can sit in the first chair. Then instruct the nurse to look under his chair and get the card taped there. The nurse must then place that card on the floor in front of the group so that everyone can see the word on the card. Then repeat, "I pray throughout the day, working at ________." Give a clue for the next occupation. (You can say where that person works or what that person does.) Ask that student to go to the second chair, having the students move down. The student with that occupation takes the card from underneath the chair and places it with the first card on the floor, but in the order of the verse. Continue in this way until all the cards are arranged in the correct order on the floor. When the game is finished, mix up the cards and let the students tape them under the chairs again to get ready for your next group.

DISCUSS: **Why do people pray? Why does God want people to pray? Why would someone pray at work? Where do you go during most days? How can you pray throughout the day?**

2. CHOOSE A PLAN

MATERIALS
prepared picnic snacks, prepared index card

Bring some snacks like those you would have on a picnic. Divide these into three bags, one bag for each of your groups. Hide these so the students don't see them. Write on an index card, "One of the main reasons so many of God's children don't have a significant life of prayer is not so much that we don't want to, but that we don't plan to" (from *Desiring God* by John Piper, Multnomah Books, 1996).

DO: As if it were a spontaneous idea, tell the students, **Hey, let's have a picnic!** Then lead them to a place in your room or another room where you can sit on the floor or outside where you can sit on the grass. Sit down as if you are at a picnic. Then look around expectantly. Give the students a little time to ask, "Where's the food?" or make other comments. Then say, "Oh. I guess picnics happen better when you plan them." Read the comment from the index card. Tell the students that we don't grow into a good relationship with God without planning to pray. Then tell the students that you actually did plan for a picnic. Bring out the snacks. While the students eat, review the "hand pattern" way of praying that the students learned in Session 3. Review the "clock" method of praying that they learned in Session 4.

DISCUSS: **Have you been using one of these methods to help you pray?** If they have, ask them how it's going. If they haven't, ask them if they are using another plan. If so, encourage them to tell about it, since it might be useful for other students. Encourage any who don't have a plan to choose a plan now. Ask them to choose a time to pray. Give them a minute to think. Then ask for volunteers to tell you when they plan to pray.

If the next group has seen that your previous group *did* have a picnic, when they sit down for the picnic and nothing is available, you may say, "Oh. I guess I should have planned for more than one group!" (or two groups).

3. PRAYER POSTURES

MATERIALS
none needed

DO: Seat the students with you in a small circle of chairs. You sit in the first chair in the circle. Ask the students to tell you some different body positions people use when they pray. Then assign these to different students. Each student will need a different posture, so you may want to suggest a few yourself. Try:

- both hands raised
- one hand raised
- hands in front with palms up as if receiving a gift
- hands folded with fingers bent and linked
- hands palm to palm with fingers straight
- kneeling
- standing
- head up
- head down
- hands covering face

Now have the students begin a rhythm of patting their laps, then clapping their hands: pat-clap-pat-clap. Start fairly slowly. After a four-count (pat-clap-pat-clap) do your posture and then someone else's posture. Everyone else keeps the pat-clap rhythm going. The person whose posture you did waits for the four-count and then does her posture and someone else's. After the next four-count, the next person does his posture and then someone else's. Continue in this way as long as you wish. For example, pat-clap-pat-clap, head up, hands up, pat-clap-pat-clap, hands up, hands covering face, and so on. If someone can't think of a posture (his own or someone else's) or gets flustered, that person goes to the end of the line and everyone else moves up. When they move up, they take the posture that formerly belonged to the person who sat in the seat they have moved to.

DISCUSS: **Does it matter what posture we use when we pray? Why would someone look up? Why would someone kneel? What prayer posture do you prefer to use?** Ask the students what their prayer plan is (if they have been to Discovery Center #2).

DISCOVERERS' DEBRIEFING

If you have time to review, gather as a large group and discuss your young discoverers' findings. Ask the following questions:

- **What is the most interesting thing you discovered today?**
- **What did you learn today that you didn't know before?**
- **Why do people pray?**
- **Why does God want us to pray?**
- **Why should we plan to pray?**
- **When is it helpful to use a prayer plan (like the hand pattern)?**
- **What kinds of postures do people use when they pray? Why?**

Review the Scripture for today.

Ask the students to pledge to pray and challenge them to keep it up.

Pray, asking God's help in remembering to pray, and in knowing what to pray. Thank God for wanting to have this relationship with us. Thank him for listening to our prayers and answering them.